BREAD BAKING FOR TEENS

SWIRLED CINNAMON RAISIN SOURDOUGH, page 114

BREAD BAKING
FOR TEENS

30 STEP-BY-STEP RECIPES
FOR BEGINNERS

Katie Shaw

Photography by Laura Flippen
Illustrations by Alyssa Nassner

**ROCKRIDGE
PRESS**

Interior and Cover Designer: Jami Spittler
Art Producer: Tom Hood
Editor: Marjorie DeWitt
Production Editor: Ellina Litmanovich
Production Manager: Jose Olivera

Photography © Laura Flippen, 2021. Illustration © Alyssa Nassner, 2021.

Paperback ISBN: 978-1-63807-445-8 | eBook ISBN: 978-1-63807-245-4
R0

FOR MADDIE, CAMILLA,
AND ELLIE:
MY FAVORITE BAKERS

CONTENTS

INTRODUCTION

I'll never forget the first loaf of bread I made. I was in college and had just moved into my first house with a real oven. I picked a recipe out of an old cookbook from my parents and got to work. At first, it seemed like such a mystery: working with yeast, figuring out the rising process, and learning how to knead. But to my surprise, it turned out perfectly. It was like magic.

I now have a serious love for making bread, and I've learned a lot since then. I still bake a loaf or two every week, and I love to experiment with new flavors: mixing chocolate chips, dried fruit, or nuts into the dough, brushing garlic butter on top, dividing loaves into rolls, and any other twists I can think of. I love everything from the feel of the dough to the look of a finished loaf to (of course) the taste of that still-warm first slice. There are so many benefits to making your bread at home: it saves money, you can control the ingredients, and you don't have to worry about the grocery store running out of your favorite kind. But truly, the best thing about baking bread is that it's fun. It's a hobby that just keeps giving.

If you're ready to start your own bread-baking adventure, you're in the right place. This book is for complete beginners. We're going to discuss the ingredients you'll need, the bread-baking process, and tips for success. You will go from bread-baking novice to pro.

Even though bread baking might seem mysterious to you at first, like it did to me, it's really a simple process. What makes bread baking different from other types of baking is the fact that bread uses yeast (instead of something like baking soda) to help it rise. This means that bread baking can take a bit longer than other baking recipes. There are also specific steps

you'll want to follow to make sure your loaves are fluffy and delicious. Don't worry—we're going to walk through each and every one of these steps together.

We'll start with a basic no-knead recipe. Your first recipe will get you comfortable working with yeast and watching the rising process. From there, we'll work our way up to some recipes that are a little fancier. We'll make some classic sandwich breads that are perfect for every day, then some rolls for special dinners. Then we will move on to sweet breads and finally to sourdoughs. Each recipe will build on what you've learned from the previous recipe, so you'll want to work your way through the book in order. Once you've mastered the basic process, you can (and will!) make everything from a simple sandwich loaf all the way up to filled and braided breads.

All baking is fun, but you'll soon find that there's something special about bread baking. I hope that this book shows you that making bread is fun and rewarding. You'll be proud to share your creations and show off your new skill. I hope this will be the beginning of a hobby that will grow with you and last a lifetime. Let's get started!

BREAD BASICS

To get started, let's review some bread-baking basics. Even if you're an experienced baker, be sure to read this chapter. Making bread is different from most other types of baking. You might not be familiar with some ingredients, and the process seems a little strange at first. Once you've read this chapter, you'll be ready to put your apron on and start baking.

THE MAIN INGREDIENTS

Four simple ingredients are the building blocks of almost every bread recipe. You can, of course, add more ingredients for flavor. Still, your foundation is flour, water, salt, and yeast.

Flour

While there are different types of flours you can choose from, flour will always be the backbone of every single loaf. Make sure you are baking with fresh flour for the best results. Check the expiration date before purchasing and store it in an airtight container. Important: Raw flour can make us sick if consumed, so be sure to wash your hands after handling dough or raw flour, and never eat raw dough.

All-purpose flour: This variety of flour is the easiest to find and is in every grocery store. It's the same flour used in most recipes for baked goods like muffins and cookies, and is also used in most of the bread recipes in this book.

Bread flour: A bit less commonly used, you'll still find bread flour in most stores. It has a higher protein content and is excellent for making crusty, chewy loaves, like Overnight No-Knead Crusty Rolls (page 47) and No-Fail Hearty White Sandwich Bread (page 52).

Whole wheat flour: Whole wheat recipes use whole wheat flour, which is higher in fiber, iron, and other nutrients. It gives whole wheat recipes a delicious flavor and a beautiful, deep color, which you'll see on Light Honey Wheat Sandwich Bread (page 54).

Water

Water helps all the ingredients blend properly and allows the flour to start developing gluten as you knead.

Yeast needs water to activate and start bubbling, which is what allows your bread to rise.

There's no need to use bottled or any other special water. In most cases, tap water will work just fine!

Salt

Without salt, your finished bread will taste flat and lack flavor. Salt also slows down the fermentation process of the yeast, which gives it enough time to develop flavor as it rises. Finally, salt helps the crust brown as it bakes.

A loaf of bread without salt will be bland, floppy, and pale, so make sure you add the correct amount and the type that the recipe calls for.

Table salt: This is typical salt that you would find in a home saltshaker. It's ideal for baking because the smaller granules dissolve easily into your dough.

Kosher salt: Kosher salt has larger crystals than table salt. It's great for topping pizzas, bagels, crusty loaves of bread, or any other time you're looking for bold flavor and texture on top of a baked good.

Yeast

Yeast may seem intimidating, but it's nothing to be nervous about! When mixed with water, yeast ferments, or consumes, any available sugars and turns them into gas. It "eats" the sugars in the flour of your dough and changes them into carbon dioxide, which gives your loaf the lovely bubbles that make it rise.

Modern yeast is very easy to work with. There are two types that are suitable for the recipes in this book.

Instant yeast: Instant yeast is excellent for beginner bread bakers. You simply mix it in your recipe with no need to proof it, activate it, or any other additional steps. Many experienced and professional bakers use instant yeast, so don't be put off by the term "instant." Instant yeast is sold in small jars next to the pouches. Sometimes you'll see it labeled as "bread machine instant yeast." You can also find it online in vacuum-sealed 1-pound pouches. It is available in grocery stores or can be purchased in bulk online.

Active dry yeast: Active dry yeast can be found just about anywhere and is typically sold in small pouches. Rising times are slightly longer than when instant yeast is used, and you will need to mix active dry yeast with liquid before adding it to your dough.

WORDS TO KNOW

There are some terms that bread bakers use that might be new to you. Because you'll read them in the recipes in this book, it's important to first understand them. It would be a great idea to review these now and refer to this section later if you run into a word you don't understand (see also page 16).

Hydration: The percentage of liquid in your recipe. More liquid means higher hydration. High-hydration doughs are a little sticky and can be harder to work with.

Knead: Somewhere between mixing and massaging, kneading dough makes it stronger and stretchier. Some recipes require it, and some don't.

Elasticity: The amount of stretchiness in your dough. As a general rule, as you knead, your dough should become smoother and more elastic.

Rise: The process of dough becoming bigger, puffier, and filled with air bubbles over time. Most recipes will call for a rise time that allows the dough to double in size.

Bulk ferment: When the dough rises the first time in a bowl or other large container.

Rest: Sometimes known as a "bench rest," the dough sits at room temperature to relax. A rest will often make the dough easier to stretch.

Proof: The final rise, after the dough is shaped into its final form. This second rise is usually a bit shorter than the bulk ferment stage.

Oven spring: When the loaf puffs up even more after hitting the heat of the oven. Most free-form loaves will have some oven spring.

BREAD STEP-BY-STEP

Most bread recipes follow the same basic process. Let's review it in depth so you're comfortable with each step before you bake your first loaf.

Scaling

Scaling means to measure out your ingredients using a scale. It might seem easier to just dump everything in a bowl right away, but it's best to measure each ingredient separately before you start combining things. Careful measuring ahead of time minimizes careless mistakes and gets you off to a good start.

WHY WEIGH?

If you have access to a kitchen scale, it will help get your flour measurement just right. There are plenty of factors that affect how much flour can fit in a measuring cup—flour containers can settle during shipping; flour can be packed into a cup tightly or loosely. One cup of flour can vary a lot! Weighing your flour ensures your recipe will come out precisely as written.

Don't have a kitchen scale? No problem at all. You might end up having to add a bit more water or a bit more flour to get the consistency of the dough just right. Each recipe will tell you when and how to do this.

Mixing

Mixing will happen in a big bowl, and you'll mix with a spatula. Every dough ingredient (except special additions such as nuts or fruits) will be added and mixed until combined. It's vital to mix before you knead to avoid a big mess on your countertop. At this stage, you'll evaluate your dough. If it seems dry and crumbly and is not coming together, you'll add a small amount of water.

If it is sticking to the bowl and not forming a ball, add a small amount of flour. At the end of this step, you should have a workable dough that's ready to knead.

Kneading and Folding

The purpose of kneading is for the dough to form gluten. Gluten is necessary for bread to have enough structure to rise. It needs strength to expand up instead of spreading out flat like a pancake.

Some recipes will use folding instead of kneading. This is a slower, gentler process that still allows the gluten to develop over time. Both are great ways to build up gluten and get a delicious loaf of bread. They're just a little different.

KNEADING

Step 1: Turn the dough out onto a clean and lightly floured surface, like a countertop or a cutting board. You want just enough flour to keep the dough from sticking. Too much will make your finished loaf too heavy. At first, the dough will be lumpy, "shaggy" looking, and slightly sticky **(see picture 1.1)**.

1.1

Step 2: Press down on the dough using the heels of your hands. Use the strength of your arms and torso as you press down **(see picture 1.2)**. Don't worry about being too hard on the dough. This should feel like a workout! Turn the dough 90 degrees and press again **(see picture 1.3)**.

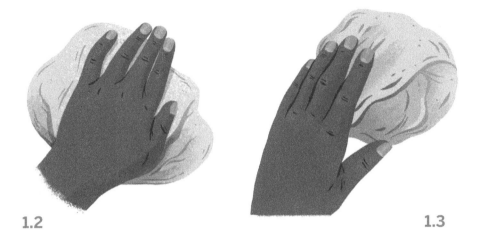

1.2   1.3

Step 3: Continue pressing and turning until the dough is smooth and stretches easily. Gently shape it into a ball for the next step **(see picture 1.4)**.

1.4

FOLDING

Step 1: Place the dough in a lightly greased bowl and gently press it down into a slightly flattened circle (see picture 2.1).

Step 2: Grasp the top of the dough and stretch it out. Fold the top of the dough down into the center of the circle, like you are closing an envelope (see picture 2.2). Do the same fold with the remaining three sides (see picture 2.3). You have now completed one fold (see picture 2.4).

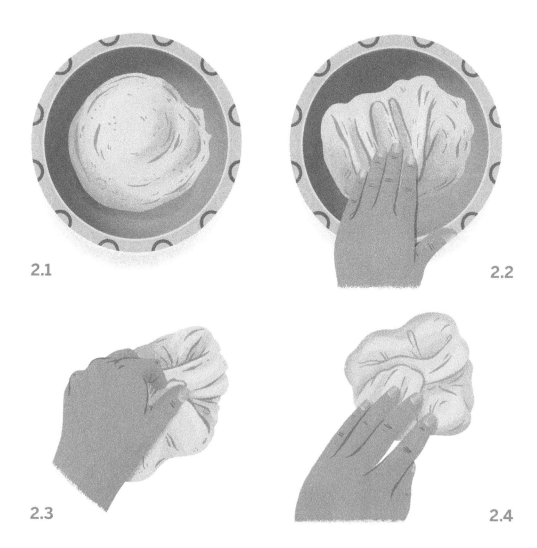

2.1

2.2

2.3

2.4

Step 3: Turn the dough over on the counter. It should look like a ball and briefly hold its shape **(see picture 2.5)**.

2.5

Rising or Bulk Fermentation

After the dough is kneaded or folded, it's time for the first rise, also known as the bulk fermentation stage. In this stage, the dough will double in size and become nice and puffy. This is when the yeast will be active, forming air bubbles that will result in a fluffy texture.

Before you set your dough aside to rise, you'll need to find a suitable place for it to go. You're looking for a warm, draft-free spot. If your home is warm (at least 80°F), the countertop will work fine. For most people, a turned-off oven will work the best.

Lightly spray a large mixing bowl with nonstick cooking spray, and place your dough inside. Cover it tightly with either a clean, damp tea towel or plastic wrap. Tuck it into the warm spot you've picked out, and let it rise. This stage will take between 45 minutes and 1 hour. The dough should be puffy and up to double the size it was when you started. If you stick your finger in the dough, it should leave an indentation.

Shaping

During the shaping phase, you will transform your dough from a puffy ball into the shape it will be when you bake it. This step will have a big effect on the look of your finished loaf. For a free-form loaf, you will simply shape the dough into a ball. For sandwich loaves, you will flatten the dough and roll it up. Each recipe will have detailed instructions about how to shape that specific dough.

It's important to know that your shaping skills will improve over time. If your first few loaves aren't perfect, don't worry! They will still taste great.

Proofing

Proofing is a second rise that takes place after shaping. This stage is important for the texture of your bread. Are you looking for a nice, high sandwich loaf or extra-fluffy rolls? That happens during the proofing phase. This will usually occur in that same warm place where bulk fermentation happened.

You'll need to take care when you cover your dough at this stage to keep it from drying out. Plastic wrap sprayed with nonstick cooking spray is a great choice. If you're doing the final proof in a turned-off oven, make sure you don't forget to move the dough before you preheat!

The proofing step is often a little shorter than bulk fermentation and is usually 1 hour or less. Each recipe will explain what your dough should look like. For most recipes, the dough will increase in volume but not double. For sandwich loaves, the bread will rise 1 to 2 inches over the top of the pan.

Scoring

Scoring is simply the act of carving a loaf with a sharp knife or lame (see page 16). This shallow cutting is done to control where a loaf splits open. In some recipes, particularly those breads you bake at higher temperatures, when they hit the heat of the oven, they will split in strange places. Scoring your dough before baking helps control where this happens. As a bonus, you can make pretty designs on your loaf. Scoring is not needed in every recipe, but it's a good technique to know.

Here's how to do it: Hold a sharp knife or lame at a 45-degree angle, and drag it across the surface of the loaf, cutting about ½ inch deep. Your first time scoring you'll want to make either one slash or an X shape. Later on, you can try more elaborate designs.

A few tips for success:

> If you want to try a design with a lot of strokes, cut only ¼ inch deep.
> You can also score before the second proof. This is easier because the dough is cooler and firmer, but the design will be less dramatic.
> A serrated knife can work in place of a lame (page 16).

Baking

The baking stage is important to get right so that the result is a loaf that is nicely browned and baked all the way through without being dry or too hard to slice.

Before preheating your oven, you'll want to arrange the racks so that you have one in the center. Remove any upper racks so that if the bread rises as it bakes, it doesn't touch an upper rack.

Sometimes a loaf will look done on the outside but not be baked through. This is normal. Be sure to follow the baking temperature and time that's given in your recipe. It's important not to remove the bread until it's done. Some people say a fully baked loaf will sound "hollow" when tapped rather than feeling dense. The best way to know if a loaf is done is by using an instant-read thermometer.

Cooling

Even though it's tempting to cut into your bread when it's fresh out of the oven, it's almost always best to wait for it to cool. Some loaves finish baking as they cool and will be gummy inside if you cut into them too early. If you are baking a sandwich loaf, letting it cool completely will give you the neatest slices and the best texture.

Dinner rolls and sweet rolls can be eaten when slightly warm, but even they benefit from at least 20 minutes of cooling.

If the recipe states to remove your bread from the pan and place it on a cooling rack to finish cooling, be sure to do so. Letting a loaf cool in the pan will make it soggy.

WHAT TO KNOW ABOUT DOUGH

There are two kinds of dough used in bread baking: straight dough and pre-ferments. It's important to know the difference, because the process for each is quite different. Recipes that use pre-ferments and starters take much longer to rise and proof, so you'll need to know which one you're doing before you plan to bake.

Straight Dough

A straight dough is made by mixing all the ingredients together during the mixing phase. It uses yeast as the rising agent. Straight doughs are easy to make and are ready relatively quickly. You can make one, from start to finish, in one afternoon.

There is a huge variety of straight dough recipes, and they are the most common. Very soft or sweet recipes, such as cinnamon rolls or brioche, are almost always straight doughs. Straight dough will also make excellent sandwich loaves and crusty breads. You can have a very fulfilling bread-baking life making only these if you choose.

Pre-Ferments and Starters

Pre-ferments and starters add one step before the bread-baking process that you have learned about in this chapter. A pre-ferment adds a deep, tangy flavor that really can't be achieved any other way. Most bread recipes that use this technique will be crusty, artisan-style loaves with great crusts, open holes, and a lot of chewiness.

While an extra step might seem like a hassle, making a starter is just a matter of planning ahead. Pre-ferments and starters are all a simple mix of flour, water, and sometimes commercial yeast that ferments overnight and then becomes an ingredient in the regular bread-baking process.

POOLISH

Poolish is a mix of water, flour, and a pinch of commercial yeast. A poolish is typically 100 percent hydration (meaning it is equal parts flour and water, measured by weight). A poolish is simply mixed up in a bowl and allowed to rest overnight. In the morning, you will have something that looks like a bubbly pancake batter.

BIGA

Think of a biga as a stiff poolish. It is two parts flour to one part water, with a pinch of yeast. It is used in the same way; it just looks different. It will look like a dough, while a poolish looks like a batter.

LEVAIN OR SOURDOUGH STARTER

This type of starter takes longer to develop (at least seven days). Rather than adding commercial yeast, you simply mix flour and water and allow it to capture wild yeast in the air. You will learn more about these in chapter 6.

LET'S GET STARTED

This chapter is your bread-baking foundation. You are going to go from interested in bread baking to making your first loaf. Once you've read this chapter, you'll bake your first loaf of bread at the end.

STUFF YOU NEED

Bread baking does require some equipment. Some tools are essential, and chances are you already have them in your kitchen. Measuring cups, measuring spoons, and a cooling rack are tools that you should have on hand for all the recipes.

Having the following items can be helpful, and as your interest in bread grows, you'll want more of the things on this list. If there is a specific item that you don't have, there are almost always workarounds.

Banneton: A lightweight, inexpensive basket that helps high-hydration dough hold its shape while it proofs. This is also called a proofing basket. You can substitute a bowl lined with a tea towel, but proofing baskets are very handy and are just the right shape. These are more important for sourdough recipes than yeast breads.

Digital scale: This allows you to measure your flour and other ingredients in grams, which is very precise.

Dutch oven: This traps moisture as your loaf bakes, helping it rise higher. If there's a Dutch oven in your home kitchen for making roasts or soups, that will do perfectly. There's no need for a special one! You can substitute a metal baking sheet with water on a lower rack to create steam.

Instant-read thermometer: This helps you know for sure that your bread is done inside. A thermometer with a pointy, narrow tip will let you check the center of your loaf and leave only a very small hole.

Lame: A supersharp blade in a special handle that allows you to score bread without any dragging. In most cases, a serrated knife will do the trick if you don't have a lame. For high-hydration breads, it's a nice tool to have.

Loaf pan: An essential pan for making sandwich breads. You'll want an 8½-by-4½-by-2 ½-inch pan for standard-size loaves.

Parchment paper: It guarantees that your bread will never stick. Parchment paper is essential when baking in a Dutch oven and very helpful for everything else. If you don't have any, you'll need to be very generous with the nonstick cooking spray and/or cornmeal on your baking sheet. For recipes with cheese or chocolate, you'll really want parchment paper for easy cleanup. Look for a package of individual sheets so you don't have to wrestle with a roll.

If you want to invest in some new tools, an instant-read thermometer will always assure you your bread is ready, and a digital scale will give you a much more precise measurement of ingredients than measuring cups and spoons. If you already own these, prepare to have them on hand for all the recipes. If not, rest assured there are workarounds.

SAFETY TIPS

Kitchen safety is important. Here are a few simple guidelines you need to follow to avoid hurting yourself or serving something that will make you or your family sick. Luckily, staying safe in the kitchen is easy! Just pay attention to these rules.

Use oven mitts. You'll be handling hot baking sheets and loaf pans. Many recipes will require you to transfer hot loaves of bread from a pan to a cooling rack, and the bread itself can burn you if you don't protect your skin.

Wash your hands. You should always wash your hands for any baking project, but with bread baking, it's essential. When you knead the dough with your hands, the very last thing you want are germs from your skin getting into the dough. Make sure your hands are spotless before you touch the dough.

Clean your countertop. Your countertop is important if you're kneading dough directly on it. It will need to be clean, and you'll need to make sure there's no residue from cleaning solutions on it. Rinse it with a wet paper towel and then dry it. You can always use a clean, heavy cutting board for kneading as well.

Tie your hair back. No one likes to find hair in food. Even worse is finding a hair kneaded into the center of a loaf! You can avoid this by simply tying your hair back before you get started.

Handle tools carefully. There are a lot of sharp objects involved with bread baking: serrated bread knives, lames, and even instant-read thermometers have a pointy end. Make sure you are careful when using sharp tools and put them away when not in use.

Keep your work area neat and clean. A messy work area is asking for mistakes to happen. Make sure you always have a clean place to set down something hot and that your counters and floors are clean and clear to avoid tripping, slipping, or breaking things.

Store leftovers properly. Homemade bread doesn't have the same preservatives as store-bought bread. This can be a good thing, but it also means you have to be more careful with your leftovers. A loaf will stay fresh a few days at room temperature, but for any longer than that, the freezer is best. If you're making a recipe that contains a filling or topping with fruit or dairy, you'll want to store it in the refrigerator.

KEEP IN MIND

There are a few things that can affect the outcome of your bread. Think of your kitchen conditions almost as an ingredient of their own. Let's take a look at how humidity and temperature affect your recipe.

Temperature

Water and flour are the main ingredients in your dough, and their individual temperatures will have a big effect on the starting temperature of your dough. To make sure your dough starts at the right temperature, make sure you adjust your water temperature according to how warm or cool your kitchen is.

WATER TEMPERATURE

As you learned in chapter 1, when yeast is mixed with water, it becomes active and causes your dough to rise. The temperature that you use in your dough can have a big effect on this. If the water is too hot, it can kill the yeast. This will result in a totally flat loaf. If the water is too cold, it will slow the rising process, because it decreases the temperature of your dough. You don't need to overthink this. Make sure your water is somewhere around room temperature, and you'll be just fine.

AIR TEMPERATURE

Once your dough is ready for the first rise, air temperature becomes a significant factor. In general, the warmer the air, the faster the dough will rise. Just like hot water, hot air can kill the yeast and ruin the loaf. The ideal place for your dough to rise is somewhere in the range of 80°F to 90°F. You can use a few tricks to create a spot in your house that's just the right temperature. You can turn on your oven for 1 to 2 minutes, then turn it off. Some people have a corner of their home that is very warm on sunny days. Another option is to put a bowl of hot water in a turned-off oven with your dough.

The ideal starting temperature of dough is 74°F. But that doesn't mean that all your ingredients have to be exactly 74°F! If your water or flour is warmer or cooler than this, simply adjust the other ingredient. Use the chart below to help you.

AIR AND FLOUR TEMPERATURE	WATER TEMPERATURE
55°F	110°F
60°F	100°F
65°F	90°F
70°F	80°F
75°F	70°F
80°F	60°F
85°F	50°F

Humidity

It's important to take account of the weather when baking. Humidity will affect your ingredients and your finished loaf. Here are a few things to look out for.

MEASURING FLOUR

You might notice that after a sudden change in the weather, your bread starts coming out differently. This can be caused by your flour absorbing moisture in the air when there is high humidity. One-hundred grams of flour may act differently when it's absorbed water prior to baking. There is a simple fix for this problem. Prepare your recipe the same way you always do, and just add a little more flour as needed.

Being able to gauge whether your dough needs a little more flour or water is a skill that will come to you quickly with practice.

MANAGING MOISTURE DURING THE BAKING PROCESS

Many beginners add too much flour during the kneading process. If the dough is so sticky you can't knead it, add just a little flour. If it is only slightly sticking to the counter or your hands, resist the urge to keep adding flour. You'll end up with a dough that has too much flour and turns out dense.

You'll need to keep your dough moist as it rises. If it gets dry, it will form a crust and stop rising. Make sure your dough is covered during the first and second rise. You can use a damp, clean tea towel or plastic wrap that's been coated with a nonstick cooking spray. It's important that your cover doesn't stick to the dough, especially during the second rise.

Time

Time is crucial in bread baking. Most recipes will take a few hours at least. Don't worry; most of this is hands-off time! Your bread needs time to rise, bake, and cool. Starters and pre-ferments need time to ferment. This can't be rushed, so don't make bread when you're in a hurry.

Altitude

Altitude is how high you are above sea level, and it can have a significant effect on baking. Higher locations have lower air pressure, which means dough will rise faster in the oven and on the counter. To counteract this, try decreasing the yeast by 25 percent in your recipe and keeping a close eye on your dough to avoid over-proofing.

WHAT IF

Not every loaf will be perfect, especially at first. Don't worry about this; you will learn something with every loaf, and every mistake will improve your skills. Luckily, there are a few very common issues, so it's easy to figure out what went wrong. Let's go over them, and you'll know what happened if something doesn't turn out how you hoped.

What if my dough is too sticky to work with? Some recipes will have stickier dough than others. None of them should be impossible to handle, though. If you find yourself faced with a super-sticky dough, let it rest covered for about 20 minutes and see if it becomes easier to handle. If it doesn't, add a little more flour. Do this slowly, about 1 tablespoon at a time.

What if my dough is not coming together? If you're trying to knead your dough and there are lots of little crumbly bits, your dough is probably too dry. Add 1 tablespoon or so of water, continue to knead the dough, and see if that helps. Be sure not to add too much water at once, or you'll have the opposite problem!

What if my dough doesn't rise? This is very often a temperature issue. Have you put your dough in a warm (but not hot) place? Is it possible that you killed the yeast with very hot water when you first mixed the ingredients? Sometimes dough will just need a little patience. If you are running into this issue repeatedly, you might have expired yeast, and it's time to replace it.

Why is my loaf flat? Your dough over-proofed, meaning it rose too long during either the first rise or (more commonly) the second rise. The yeast ran out of energy, and the loaf collapsed during baking. Next time, you will need to lower the temperature of the area where the dough is proofing or proof it for less time.

What if my crust is pale? Pale crust and a flat loaf can show up at the same time because they are both caused by over-proofed dough. In most cases, your bread will still taste great! If you find that you prefer a very brown crust, you can always brush on milk or a beaten egg before baking, just to improve the look of your loaves.

What if my bread is misshapen? If you're baking a round, free-form loaf, try deeply slashing the dough next time before baking. This allows steam to escape where you choose so that it keeps its shape better. If your rolls or sandwich loaves look a bit off, you probably just need more shaping practice.

What if the texture is dense? Dense bread is usually caused by a rising issue. Most commonly, your dough didn't get enough time to rise during the first or second rise. Sometimes, the bread will be dense because it rose for too long, and the yeast ran out of energy, so to speak. How can you tell the difference? Over-risen bread will typically look like it collapsed. Under-risen bread will look like it never got big enough.

What if my bread is gummy inside? This happens when bread is under-baked or undercooled. If you've taken your bread out of the oven too soon, it's too late to save the loaf. If it's cool and unbaked in the center, it is not safe to consume. But if you cut into a loaf when it's still hot, and it looks undone in the center, that's okay. Give it more time to cool, and it might improve in a few hours.

Your First Recipe:
No-Knead Rustic White Bread

Yield 1 loaf Prep 10 minutes Inactive 11 hours Bake 40 minutes

This recipe is a no-knead bread and is the perfect starting point for beginners. After making this bread, you'll be comfortable working with yeast and will understand all the steps of bread baking.

Throughout this book, the recipes will increase in difficulty. As you make them, you will increase in skill. You'll want to work through the chapters in order.

Your journey starts here, with an easy loaf that you'll be proud to serve. Instead of being kneaded, this dough rests on the counter, and gluten develops in it over time. The taste and texture are just as good as a kneaded loaf.

TOOLS:		
Large mixing bowl Rubber spatula	Plastic wrap Parchment paper	Baking sheet Sharp knife or lame

3¼ cups (400 grams) all-purpose flour 1½ teaspoons salt	1 teaspoon yeast, instant or active dry	1 cup plus 1 tablespoon water, divided Nonstick cooking spray

1. **Mix the ingredients.** In a large mixing bowl, combine the flour, salt, and yeast. Add 1 cup of water. Mix well with a spatula. If you notice dry bits of dough, add the remaining 1 tablespoon of water and continue to mix. The dough should form a ball, but it will still look very rough and lumpy.

2. **The first rise.** Tightly cover the bowl of dough with plastic wrap. Place the covered bowl on the counter at room temperature, and leave it to rise for 10 hours or overnight. Because this recipe is no-knead, this long rise is necessary. Be sure to leave it for the full

continued ▶

10 hours. At the end of the rise time, the dough should be very puffy and should have doubled in size. When you poke it with your finger, your finger should leave an indentation that fills slowly. If the dough is still very firm or has not changed much in size, give it more time.

3. Shape into a ball. Prepare a baking sheet by lining it with parchment paper or spraying it generously with nonstick cooking spray. Gently pick the dough out of the bowl, and shape it into a smooth ball. When you pull and pinch the bottom of the dough, it pulls the top of the ball tight. You will see the ball become round and smooth on top as you pinch. Never smash down from the top to shape, or your dough will be flat and dense. Place the dough onto the prepared baking sheet. Using a very sharp knife or lame, make an X-shaped slash in the center of the loaf, cutting around ¼ inch deep.

4. The second rise. Prepare a warm place for the second rise, either by briefly turning on your oven or placing a bowl of hot water inside it. Cover the ball of dough with greased plastic wrap, making sure that it is completely covered. Allow the dough to rise for about 45 minutes, until puffy but not quite doubled in size. Toward the end of the rising time, preheat your oven to 425°F with the rack in the center of the oven, taking care to remove the dough first.

5. Bake. Bake the loaf for 35 to 40 minutes. The finished loaf will be deep golden brown and have an internal temperature of 200°F. Remove the bread from the baking sheet and place it on a cooling rack. Allow the bread to cool for at least 15 minutes before serving.

EAT IT! Serve alongside a dish of olive oil, dried basil, and a splash of balsamic vinegar for dipping to make any dinner feel special.

TRY THIS! You can experiment with different designs for slashing your bread. Try an initial, a heart, or a zigzag pattern.

QUICK AND NO-KNEAD BREADS

These bread recipes are beginner friendly for one big reason: there's no kneading required! Making bread is truly as simple as mixing and waiting. Okay, there's a *little* more to it.

You can't rush these recipes; the long rising times take the place of the kneading process. If you don't mind a little planning ahead, these are a perfect choice. You'll find focaccia, flatbread, ultra-easy pizza dough, and plenty of rustic breads in this chapter.

Even though these are very easy to make, don't underestimate them: they are satisfying to make and delicious to eat. You'll turn back to these recipes long after you've mastered more complicated techniques.

Easy Make-Ahead No-Knead Pizza Dough

Yield 1 pie Prep 10 minutes, plus 25 minutes to shape and dress pizza
Inactive 11 hours Bake 20 minutes

Homemade pizza is one of the easiest dinners to make if you have the dough ready to go. This recipe takes a little planning, because you mix it up the day before, but it takes just a few minutes of work. Volunteer to oversee pizza night once or twice a month to earn some brownie points!

TOOLS:		
Large mixing bowl Rubber spatula	Plastic wrap Parchment paper	Baking sheet or pizza stone
2½ cups (395 grams) all-purpose flour	1 teaspoon (4 grams) sugar	1 teaspoon yeast, instant or active dry
1 cup plus 1 tablespoon water	1 tablespoon (14 grams) olive oil, plus extra for oiling the bowl	
1½ teaspoons salt		

1. **Mix the ingredients.** In a large mixing bowl, combine the flour, water, salt, sugar, oil, and yeast. Mix well with a spatula, incorporating any dry areas of flour. The dough should form a ball. It will look rough and shaggy at first. Wash out the mixing bowl and lightly rub or brush with olive oil. Place the pizza dough back inside the bowl.

2. **Cover the dough and allow it to rise.** Tightly cover the bowl of dough with plastic wrap. Place the covered bowl in the refrigerator, and allow it to rise for 10 hours or overnight. This dough can be left in the refrigerator for up to 24 hours if it is tightly covered. In the morning, check the dough to see if it has doubled in size. If the dough has not changed much in size, remove it from the refrigerator and give it more time to rise on the counter.

3. **Rest.** Remove the dough from the bowl and place it on a lightly floured counter. Sprinkle with flour. Cover the dough with a damp tea towel or plastic wrap. (It is okay to use the same plastic wrap from step 2.) Allow it to come to room temperature so it will be stretchier and easy to handle. This will take about 1 hour, depending on the temperature of your kitchen.

4. **Bake.** To bake into a pizza, line a rimmed baking sheet with parchment paper and stretch the dough out into a rectangle. Layer with pizza sauce and shredded mozzarella cheese. Bake at 425°F for 17 to 20 minutes, until the edges are golden brown and the center of the pizza is baked through. The pizza dough will bubble up slightly as it bakes. Transfer the whole pizza to a cooling rack to cool for 5 minutes before slicing. It's easiest to cut it into squares for serving.

TRY THIS! You can use pizza dough for more than a pizza. Try making pizza rolls by layering 1½ cups of shredded mozzarella and covering it with one layer of sliced pepperoni. Roll it up into a log, tuck the ends under, and bake for 40 minutes at 375°F. Let it cool for 10 minutes and slice for a delicious snack or appetizer.

EAT IT! If you like crisp, thin-crust pizza, you can make it with this recipe. Divide the dough in half as soon as it comes out of the refrigerator. Stretch the dough into two 13-inch rounds on top of parchment paper. If the dough tears, let it rest covered on the counter until you can stretch it thin. Top with sauce, cheese, and any other toppings you like. For an extra-crispy crust, preheat a pizza stone for 30 minutes at 450°F. Using a heatproof cutting board, carefully slide the parchment paper and the pizza onto the stone. Bake for 11 minutes.

One-Bowl Focaccia

Yield 1 loaf Prep 10 minutes Inactive 11 hours Bake 30 minutes

This is one of the most straightforward recipes in this book: there's no shaping necessary, you only get one bowl dirty, and you only need a few minutes of mixing time. In the summertime, you can make a whole meal just out of focaccia, a few slices of cheese, and fresh veggies. It's perfect for a lazy day.

TOOLS:		
Large mixing bowl Rubber spatula	Plastic wrap Parchment paper	9-by-13-inch baking dish

4 cups (500 grams)
  all-purpose flour
	1½ cups plus
	  2 tablespoons water
		1½ teaspoons yeast,
		  instant or active dry

2 tablespoons
  (28 grams) butter
	1 teaspoon (4 grams)
	  sugar
		Nonstick cooking spray

¼ cup (54 grams) olive oil	2 teaspoons salt	

1. **Mix the ingredients.** In a large mixing bowl, combine the flour, butter, oil, water, sugar, salt, and yeast. Mix well with a spatula until all ingredients are incorporated. The dough will be sticky and slightly rough looking.

2. **The first rise.** Tightly cover the bowl of dough with plastic wrap. Place the covered bowl in the refrigerator for 10 hours or overnight for the first rise. If the dough has not risen much in the morning, place it on the counter until it has doubled in size.

3. **Stretch into a rectangle.** Lightly coat a 9-by-13-inch baking dish with cooking spray or line it with parchment paper. Gently remove the dough from the mixing bowl, deflating any large air bubbles. Stretch it out into a rectangle that's the full size of the dish. If the dough keeps snapping back and doesn't stretch out easily, let it rest covered for 10 minutes and try again.

4. **The second rise.** Cover the dough with plastic wrap and place it in a warm place, such as an oven that has been briefly turned on. Allow the flatbread to rise for about 30 minutes, until it is starting to bubble up again. It does not need to double in size. Toward the end of the rising time, remove the dough from the oven.

5. **Bake and cool.** Preheat the oven to 400°F with a rack in the center. Remove the plastic wrap, and bake the loaf for 30 minutes, until golden brown and about 195°F in the center. When the bread is done, place the baking dish on a cooling rack, and let the flatbread cool right in the pan. Cut into squares and eat.

EAT IT! Flatbread is much more versatile than you might think. You can use it as sandwich bread slices or top a slice with tomato sauce and cheese for a quick pizza.

KNEAD HELP? If the dough seems stiff when you first remove it from the refrigerator, don't worry. As it warms up on the counter, it will become easier to work with. If you're still having a hard time stretching it flat to cover the baking sheet, shape it into a rough rectangle and let it rest covered for 15 minutes before stretching it out more.

TRY THIS! For an Italian twist on this recipe, sprinkle garlic powder and Italian seasoning on top just before baking.

No-Knead Holiday Cranberry Walnut Loaf

Yield 1 loaf Prep 10 minutes Inactive 12 hours Bake 40 minutes

Cranberry and walnut are the perfect flavor combination for late fall and winter. This recipe is ideal when you need a cozy wintertime treat that's easy to make. It's also a lovely homemade gift. Wrap the loaf up in parchment paper, tie it with twine, and deliver it to a friend or bring it to Thanksgiving dinner.

TOOLS:		
Small bowl Strainer Large mixing bowl	Rubber spatula Plastic wrap Parchment paper	Baking sheet Sharp knife or lame

⅓ cup (75 grams) dried cranberries 1 cup plus 3 tablespoons water, plus more for soaking dried cranberries	3¼ cups plus 2 tablespoons (425 grams) all-purpose flour 1½ teaspoons salt 1 tablespoon (12 grams) granulated sugar	½ teaspoon yeast, instant or active dry ½ cup (75 grams) coarsely chopped walnuts Nonstick cooking spray

1. **Soak the dried cranberries.** Place the dried cranberries in a small bowl, and fill the bowl with warm water. Dried fruit will start pulling moisture out of the dough unless it is hydrated first, so don't skip this step or you'll have dry areas in your loaf. Soak the dried cranberries for 10 minutes, then drain the water from the cranberries using a strainer or colander. There is no need to dry them; just remove the excess liquid.

2. **Mix the ingredients.** In a large mixing bowl, combine the flour, salt, sugar, and yeast. Add the walnuts, cranberries, and water. Mix well with a spatula, incorporating any dry areas of flour. The dough should

continued ▶

form a ball, but it will still look very rough and lumpy. You might see some streaking from the cranberries as you mix, but this won't be visible in the finished bread.

3. **The first rise.** Tightly cover the bowl of dough with plastic wrap. Place the covered bowl on the counter at room temperature, and leave it to rise for 10 hours or overnight. At the end of the rise time, the dough should be very puffy and should have doubled in size. When you poke it with your finger, your finger should leave an indentation that fills slowly. If the dough has not changed much in size, give it more time. A cold room will make the dough take longer to rise.

4. **Shape into a ball.** Prepare a baking sheet by lining it with parchment paper or coating it generously with cooking spray. Gently pick the dough out of the bowl, deflate any large air bubbles that have formed, and shape it into a smooth ball. When you pull and pinch the bottom of the dough, it pulls the top of the ball tight. You will see the ball become round and smooth on top as you pinch. Never smash down on the balls from the top to shape them, or they will be flat and dense. Place the dough onto the prepared baking sheet. Using a very sharp knife or lame, make a slash in the center of the loaf, cutting around ¼ inch deep.

5. **The second rise.** Prepare a warm place for the second rise, either by briefly turning on your oven or placing a bowl of hot water inside it. Cover the ball of dough with greased plastic wrap, making sure that the loaf is completely covered. Let it rise for about 45 minutes, or until the dough is puffy but not quite doubled in size. Toward the end of the rising time, remove the dough from the oven.

6. **Bake and cool.** Preheat the oven to 425°F with a rack in the center. Bake the loaf for 35 to 40 minutes. The finished loaf will be deep golden brown and have an internal temperature of 200°F. Because of the sugar in this recipe, it may seem darker than other breads you have made. Some cranberries near the surface may have burst; this

is fine. Remove the bread from the baking sheet and place it on a cooling rack. Allow the bread to cool at least 15 minutes before serving. If you are slicing the loaf, allow it to cool for at least 1 hour.

EAT IT! This makes a surprisingly good sandwich bread even though it's on the sweeter side! Try slicing it and making a sandwich with turkey and sharp cheddar. Or, cut thick slices and use them as a base for your favorite French toast recipe.

TRY THIS! Brush an egg wash and sprinkle sugar on top before baking for a shiny, sweet loaf. Mix 1 egg and 1 tablespoon of water in a small mixing bowl and gently brush on before baking. Sprinkle with coarse granulated sugar. For a different flavor, substitute raisins for half or all of the cranberries.

Cheddar and Jalapeño
No-Knead Bread

Yield 1 loaf Prep 10 minutes Inactive 12 hours Bake 40 minutes

Cheddar and jalapeño are a match made in heaven. When you're looking for something that's just a little different, try this spicy loaf. I love to make a few loaves in the summer, when jalapeños are in season, and freeze them for cooler fall days.

TOOLS:		
Large mixing bowl Rubber spatula	Plastic wrap Parchment paper	Baking sheet Sharp knife or lame

⅓ cup chopped jalapeños (pickled or fresh are both fine; be sure to use gloves while handling hot peppers and wash your hands immediately afterward), plus more for topping	3¼ cups plus 2 tablespoons (425 grams) all-purpose flour 1 cup plus 3 tablespoons water 1½ teaspoons salt 1 teaspoon (4 grams) sugar	½ teaspoon yeast, instant or active dry ⅓ cup diced cheddar cheese, cut into ½-inch cubes Nonstick cooking spray

1. **Mix the ingredients.** If you're using pickled jalapeños, be sure to drain any excess liquid. In a large mixing bowl, combine the flour, water, salt, sugar, yeast, jalapeños, and cheese. It's important to mix everything together at once so that the cheese and peppers will distribute evenly. Mix well with a spatula, incorporating any dry areas of flour. The dough should form a shaggy ball. If there are any dry bits that are not incorporating, add a few more teaspoons of water and continue to mix.

2. **The first rise.** Tightly cover the bowl of dough with plastic wrap. Place the covered bowl in the refrigerator and allow it to rise for 10 hours or overnight. In the morning, check the dough to see if it has nearly doubled in size. If the dough has not changed much in size, remove it from the refrigerator and give it more time to rise on the counter.

3. **Shape into a ball.** Line a baking sheet with parchment paper or coat it generously with cooking spray. This bread can really stick to the pan as the cheese melts, so parchment paper is preferred. Gently pick the dough out of the bowl, deflate any large air bubbles that have formed, and shape it into a smooth ball. When you pull and pinch the bottom of the dough, it pulls the top of the ball tight. You will see the ball become round and smooth on top as you pinch. Never smash down from the top to shape or it will be flat and dense. Place the dough onto the prepared baking sheet. To elevate your loaf, sprinkle with flour and place slices of jalapeño on top. Using a very sharp knife or lame, make a slash in the center of the loaf, cutting around ¼ inch deep.

4. **The second rise.** Prepare a warm place for the second rise, either by briefly turning on your oven or placing a bowl of hot water inside it. Cover the ball of dough with greased plastic wrap, making sure that it is completely covered. Allow the dough to rise for about 45 minutes, until puffy but not quite doubled in size. Toward the end of the rising time, remove the dough from the oven.

5. **Bake and cool.** Preheat the oven to 425°F with a rack in the center. Bake the loaf for 35 to 40 minutes, or until the loaf is a deep golden brown and has an internal temperature of 200°F. Some cheese may have leaked from the loaf, but don't worry, most will still be inside. Carefully remove the bread from the baking sheet and place it on a

continued ▶

cooling rack. Allow the bread to cool for at least 40 minutes before serving. If you cut into the loaf too soon, the cheese can leak out.

DON'T HAVE IT? If you don't have jalapeño peppers (or aren't a fan!), you can substitute diced green bell peppers or just leave them out.

EAT IT! This bread pairs perfectly with chili, stew, or a hearty soup. You might want to serve it with something on the mild side to offset the spice. If you want to try this as sandwich bread, try a jalapeño popper grilled cheese: spread the bread with cream cheese, add some cheddar and bacon, and cook in a pan on the stovetop. Trust me, it's delicious!

TRY THIS! For an Italian-inspired twist on this recipe, substitute cubed mozzarella or provolone for the cheddar and drained, chopped roasted red peppers for the jalapeños.

No-Knead Cheesy Flatbread

Yield 1 large flatbread Prep 15 minutes Inactive 11 hours Bake 30 minutes

I started making this flatbread as a portable version of grilled cheese. You can bake it in the morning and cut it into squares. Pack a thermos of tomato soup, and you have the perfect homemade lunch you can eat anywhere.

TOOLS:		
Large mixing bowl Rubber spatula	Plastic wrap Parchment paper	9-by-13-inch baking dish

3 cups (375 grams)
  all-purpose flour
2 tablespoons
  (28 grams) olive oil
1⅓ cups water
1 teaspoon salt
	1 teaspoon yeast,
	  instant or active dry
	2 tablespoons shred-
	  ded or grated
	  Parmesan cheese
		1½ cups diced cheddar
		  cheese
		Nonstick cooking spray

1. **Mix the ingredients.** In a large mixing bowl, combine the flour, oil, water, salt, yeast, and both types of cheese. Mix well with a spatula until all ingredients are incorporated. The dough will be sticky and slightly rough looking.

2. **The first rise.** Tightly cover the bowl of dough with plastic wrap. Place the covered bowl in the refrigerator overnight for the first rise. In the morning, if the dough has not risen much, place it on the counter until it has doubled in size.

3. **Stretch into a rectangle.** Coat a 9-by-13-inch pan with cooking spray or line it with parchment paper. (Any recipe with cheese is more likely to stick, so use parchment paper if you have it.) Gently transfer the dough to the pan, deflating any large air bubbles. Stretch the dough into a rectangle that's the full size of the pan. If the dough

continued ▶

keeps snapping back and doesn't stretch out easily, let it rest covered for 10 minutes and try again.

4. **The second rise.** Cover the pan with plastic wrap and put it in a warm place, such as an oven that has been briefly turned on. Allow the dough to rise for about 30 minutes, or until it is starting to bubble up again. It does not need to double in size. Toward the end of the rising time, remove the dough from the oven.

5. **Bake and cool.** Preheat the oven to 400°F with a rack in the center. Remove the plastic wrap, and bake the loaf for 30 minutes, or until golden brown and about 195°F in the center. It will puff up as it bakes. When the bread is done, place the pan on a cooling rack and let the flatbread cool right in the pan. Cut into squares and eat.

TRY THIS! You can add just about anything to flatbread! Try 1 tablespoon of dried herbs, 2 tablespoons of drained sun-dried tomatoes, and 2 tablespoons of coarsely chopped olives.

EAT IT! Cut the flatbread into small squares and serve with hummus or an olive tapenade for a Mediterranean-inspired appetizer.

No-Knead Hearty Oatmeal Bread

Yield 1 loaf   Prep 20 minutes   Inactive 13 hours   Bake 40 minutes

Yes, you can make no-knead sandwich bread! This recipe uses oats for extra flavor and texture. When you cut into it, you'll be amazed by how light and soft it is, all without a single minute spent kneading.

TOOLS:		
Large mixing bowl Rubber spatula	Plastic wrap	8½-by-4½-by- 2½-inch loaf pan

1 cup plus
  3 tablespoons hot
  water
2 tablespoons
  (28 grams) butter
	½ cup old-fashioned
	  oats
	2½ cups (300 grams)
	  all-purpose flour
	2 tablespoons
	  (25 grams) sugar
		1½ teaspoons salt
		1 teaspoon yeast,
		  instant or active dry
		Nonstick cooking spray

1. **Mix the oats and water.** In a large mixing bowl, combine the hot water, butter, and oats. Mix well, and allow the mixture to cool, uncovered, on the counter, until warm but not hot. This will take at least 15 minutes. If you add the remaining ingredients while the water is still hot, you will kill the yeast.

2. **Add the remaining ingredients.** Once the oats have cooled down enough, add the flour, sugar, salt, and yeast. Mix well to form a rough, shaggy dough. The oats will make the dough look extra lumpy, but this is normal.

3. **The first rise.** Tightly cover the bowl of dough with plastic wrap. Place the covered bowl on the counter at room temperature, and allow it to rise for 10 hours or overnight. In the morning, the dough should be very bubbly and should have doubled in size. If it has not, give it a bit more time.

continued ▶

4. **Deflate and shape.** Gently reshape the dough into a ball and deflate the air bubbles. Coat the loaf pan with cooking spray. Gently stretch the dough into a rectangle. Use your loaf pan as your guide to make the short side of the rectangle the same length as the longer side of the loaf pan. The rectangle will be about 9 by 18 inches. Tuck in the corners and start to roll in the top of the dough. Think of the saying "shoulders in, head down." Roll the dough into a log. Tuck the ends under. Pinch the seams closed, and place the loaf, seam-side down, into the loaf pan.

5. **The second rise.** Prepare a warm place for the second rise, either by briefly turning on your oven or placing a bowl of hot water inside it. Cover the pan with greased plastic wrap to prevent sticking. Allow the dough to rise for 35 to 45 minutes, until it is 1 inch over the top of the pan. Toward the end of the rising time, remove the dough from the oven.

6. **Bake and cool.** Preheat the oven to 350°F. Remove the plastic wrap and bake the loaf for 40 minutes, or until golden brown and about 195°F in the center. When the bread is done, carefully remove it from the loaf pan and place it on a wire cooling rack. If you're slicing it for sandwiches, you will get the neatest slices if you let it cool completely for at least a few hours.

7. **Store.** This loaf will stay fresh, tightly wrapped, at room temperature for 2 to 3 days. To store it longer, place a fully cooled loaf in an extra-large freezer bag.

Olive Oil and Rosemary No-Knead Bread

Yield 1 loaf   Prep 10 minutes   Inactive 11 hours   Bake 40 minutes

Ever been to a restaurant where one of the best things is the bread? This recipe is inspired by one of my family's favorite Italian restaurants, where we only order dishes that come with this bread on the side. You'll love it alongside a big plate of pasta or served with a salad.

TOOLS:		
Large mixing bowl Rubber spatula	Plastic wrap Parchment paper	Baking sheet Sharp knife or lame

3¼ cups plus 2 tablespoons (425 grams) all-purpose flour 1 cup plus 2 tablespoons water	1½ teaspoons salt 2 tablespoons (28 grams) olive oil 2 tablespoons chopped rosemary	½ teaspoon yeast, instant or active dry Nonstick cooking spray Kosher salt or large- flake sea salt for sprinkling

1. **Mix the ingredients.** In a large mixing bowl, combine the flour, water, salt, oil, rosemary, and yeast. Mix well with a spatula, incorporating any dry areas of flour. As you stir, the dough should form a ball. It will be rough looking and slightly sticky. If it seems dry, add more water, 1 teaspoon or so at a time, and continue to mix. If it is so sticky that it is acting like a batter and not forming a ball, add a sprinkle of flour and stir again until it comes together.

2. **The first rise.** Tightly cover the bowl of dough with plastic wrap. Place the covered bowl on the counter at room temperature, and leave it to rise for 10 hours or overnight. Because this dough contains olive oil, it will rise a bit slower than a recipe without any oil or butter. At the end of the rise time, the dough should be very puffy and should have doubled in size. When you poke it with your finger, your finger

continued ▶

should leave an indentation that fills slowly. If the dough has not changed much in size, give it more time. A cold room will make the dough take longer to rise.

3. **Shape into a ball.** Prepare a baking sheet by lining it with parchment paper or coating it generously with cooking spray. Gently pick the dough out of the bowl, deflate any large air bubbles that have formed, and shape it into a smooth ball. When you pull and pinch the bottom of the dough, it pulls the top of the ball tight. You will see the ball become round and smooth on top as you pinch. Never smash down on the balls from the top to shape them, or they will be flat and dense. Place the dough onto the prepared baking sheet. Using a very sharp knife or lame, make a slash in the center of the loaf, cutting around ¼ inch deep.

4. **The second rise.** Prepare a warm place for the second rise, either by briefly turning on your oven or placing a bowl of hot water inside it. Cover the ball of dough with greased plastic wrap, making sure that the loaf is completely covered. Let it rise for about 45 minutes, or until puffy but not quite doubled in size. Toward the end of the rising time, remove the dough from the oven.

5. **Bake and cool.** Preheat the oven to 425°F with a rack in the center. Sprinkle the dough with kosher salt. Press the salt on very gently, just enough to have it stick. Be careful not to squish down the loaf. Bake for 35 to 40 minutes. The finished bread will be deep golden brown and have an internal temperature of 200°F. Remove the bread from the baking sheet and place it on a cooling rack. Allow the bread to cool for at least 15 minutes before serving. This bread is very good served warm with dinner.

DON'T HAVE IT? Don't have rosemary? You can add any dried herb instead. Basil, oregano, or an Italian seasoning blend are all good choices. Fresh herbs are tricky in baked goods and can actually turn black in the oven! Stick with dried herbs.

TRY THIS! You can add Parmesan cheese to the dough at the same time you add the herbs, but if you do, have the dough rise in the refrigerator for the first rise instead of the counter to avoid having the cheese sit out at room temperature for too long.

EAT IT! Slice this loaf vertically to use as bread for a panini. Layer on salami, provolone, and a few fresh basil leaves, and cook on a griddle or hot oiled skillet until the bread browns and the cheese melts. Put the sandwich on a plate, and let it cool for a few minutes before cutting into triangles.

Overnight No-Knead Crusty Rolls

Yield 8 rolls Prep 20 minutes Inactive 11 hours Bake 18 minutes

Once you see how easy these rolls are, you'll never want store-bought ones again. Rolls are some of the most versatile bread items: you'll love them for sandwiches or served hot with dinner. Don't be nervous about shaping them; you'll get better each time you make this recipe.

TOOLS:		
Large mixing bowl Rubber spatula	Plastic wrap Sharp knife	Parchment paper Baking sheet

4 cups (500 grams)
  bread flour
1½ cups plus
  1 tablespoon water,
  divided

1¾ teaspoons salt
1 teaspoon (4 grams)
  granulated sugar
1 teaspoon yeast,
  instant or active dry

Nonstick cooking spray

1. **Mix the ingredients.** In a large mixing bowl, combine the flour, 1½ cups water, salt, sugar, and yeast. Mix well with a spatula, incorporating any dry areas of flour. The dough should form a ball. Bread flour absorbs more water than all-purpose flour, and the amount of water needed to hydrate it can vary between brands. If your dough still has dry bits that are not being incorporated easily, add more water 1 tablespoon at a time, and continue mixing.

2. **The first rise.** Tightly cover the bowl of dough with plastic wrap. Place the covered bowl on the counter at room temperature and allow it to rise for 10 hours or overnight. In the morning, the dough should be very large and bubbly. If not, give it more time until it has doubled in size.

3. **Divide and shape into rolls.** Line a baking sheet with parchment paper or coat it generously with cooking spray. Gently pick the dough

continued ▶

out of the bowl and shape it into a smooth log, deflating any large air bubbles. Using a sharp knife, divide the dough into eight equal pieces. It's easiest to first divide it in half, then quarters, then eighths. If you want the rolls to be exactly the same size, you can weigh the dough in grams before you divide it, divide that number by eight, and make each roll equal to that. Pick up one ball of dough and pinch the bottom to pull the top of the roll tight. You will see the roll become round and smooth on top as you pinch. Never smash down on the rolls from the top to shape them, or they will be flat and dense. The less you handle the dough, the better the rolls will be, so try to shape them and place them down gently. Arrange the rolls onto the baking sheet, evenly spaced.

4. **The second rise.** Prepare a warm place for the second rise, either by briefly turning on your oven or placing a bowl of hot water inside it. Lightly cover the rolls with heavily greased plastic wrap. If plastic wrap sticks to them, they will not look nice when baked, so take care to really spray your wrap. Allow them to rise in a warm place for about 30 to 40 minutes, until puffy but not quite doubled in size. Rolls rise much faster than whole loaves, so keep an eye on them or set a timer to check them. Toward the end of the rising time, preheat the oven to 450°F with the rack in the center.

5. **Bake.** Place the baking sheet on the center rack of the oven, and bake the rolls for 15 to 18 minutes, or until they are golden brown on the top and underneath and 195°F in the center. Carefully place the rolls on a wire cooling rack for at least 15 minutes before serving. Store in an airtight bag for up to 3 days at room temperature. To freeze the rolls, allow them to cool fully. Store them in a freezer bag for up to 1 month. Defrost in the microwave for 1 minute on the defrost setting.

TRY THIS! Want to make your rolls extra pretty? Before baking, brush with an egg wash of a beaten egg and sprinkle something on top. Poppy seeds, sesame seeds, or some coarse sea salt would be a beautiful addition.

EAT IT! These are amazing for breakfast sandwiches. If you wake up early enough to shape and bake the rolls, you can have a very special breakfast for yourself. Top with a fried egg, a few slices of bacon, and a slice of cheese. Wrap the whole sandwich up in foil, and you'll have breakfast to go. Of course, these rolls are perfect for any sandwich, any time of day, as well as serving alongside dinner with some soft butter.

KNEADED BREADS

These versatile and classic kneaded bread recipes are everyday favorites that can replace almost all bread you buy at the grocery store. Because they rely on traditional kneading, these loaves are ready much faster than the recipes in the previous chapter. Most of these can be made at lunch and enjoyed with dinner.

We will explore simple sandwich loaves, soft dinner buns, and crusty baguettes. As you work your way through these recipes, you'll learn how to shape different types of rolls and loaves and master your kneading technique. Let's dive in!

No-Fail Hearty White Sandwich Bread

Yield 1 loaf Prep 20 minutes Inactive 3 hours Bake 40 minutes

Here's a recipe you could make a few times a week for the rest of your life and never get tired of eating. Perfect for everything from your morning toast to a peanut butter sandwich, this recipe will be one of your staple breads. Try slicing a loaf and freezing it so you can have homemade bread anytime.

TOOLS:		

Large mixing bowl
Rubber spatula
	Electric stand mixer
	  (optional)
	Plastic wrap
		8½-by-4½-by-
		  2½-inch loaf pan

2¾ cups (360 grams)
  bread flour
1 cup lukewarm water
	2 tablespoons
	  (28 grams) softened
	  butter
	1 tablespoon
	  (12 grams) sugar
		1¼ teaspoons salt
		2 teaspoons yeast,
		  instant or active dry
		Nonstick cooking spray

1. **Mix the ingredients.** In a large mixing bowl or the bowl of an electric stand mixer, add the flour, water, butter, sugar, salt, and yeast. Mix until a dough forms that holds together and does not stick to the sides or bottom of the bowl. If the dough seems too dry and crumbly, add more water 1 teaspoon at a time. If it's too sticky, add more flour.

2. **Knead the dough.** *To knead the dough by hand*, prepare a clean counter by lightly sprinkling it with flour. Turn the dough out onto the surface. Push down on the dough with the heel of your hand, then pick it up, fold it loosely, and push down again. Repeat this action, and after a few minutes, you will develop a rhythm. The dough will become smoother and stretchier as you knead. Knead for 10 to 15 minutes, until the dough is smooth and soft and reaches the windowpane stage (meaning that when you stretch the dough, a translucent area appears). *To knead in a stand mixer*, fit the mixer

with the hook attachment, place the dough in the bowl, and let the machine run on low for 5 to 7 minutes. If the motor gets hot, turn off the machine and let it rest for a few minutes.

3. **The first rise.** Shape the dough gently into a ball and place it inside a clean, lightly oiled bowl. (It can be the same one you mixed the dough in, as long as you wash it out first.) Cover the dough with a clean, damp tea towel and put it in a warm place to rise. Let it rise for 1 hour, or until it is puffy and has doubled in size.

4. **Shape into a loaf.** Coat the loaf pan with cooking spray. Gently stretch the dough into a rectangle. Use your loaf pan as your guide to make the short side of the rectangle the same length as the longer side of the loaf pan. The rectangle will be about 9 by 18 inches. Tuck in the corners and start to roll in the top of the dough. Roll the dough into a log. Tuck the ends under. Pinch the seams closed, and place the loaf, seam-side down, into the loaf pan.

5. **The second rise.** Cover the dough with heavily greased plastic wrap and put it in a warm place until it rises to be 1 inch above the top of the loaf pan. Toward the end of the rising time, preheat the oven to 350°F. Generously dust the top of the loaf with flour.

6. **Bake and cool.** Bake for 35 to 40 minutes, until the bread is golden brown on top and has reached 190°F to 200°F in the center. Remove it from the loaf pan and allow it to cool fully on a wire rack. If you are slicing the bread for sandwiches, let it cool for at least 3 hours for the neatest slices.

DON'T HAVE IT? If you don't have bread flour, all-purpose flour will work fine! You might need to add a little more flour, and the bread will have a slightly less hearty texture, but it will be delicious.

EAT IT! This versatile recipe is great with just about anything. For a quick and easy breakfast, try toasting a few slices, spreading it with butter, and sprinkling it with cinnamon sugar.

Light Honey Wheat Sandwich Bread

Yield 1 loaf Prep 20 minutes Inactive 2 hours 30 minutes
Bake 40 minutes

The bread combines the best of both worlds: light and fluffy white flour with hearty and flavorful whole wheat flour. Honey makes any recipe feel just a bit more wholesome. It's perfect for a homemade sandwich.

TOOLS:		
Large mixing bowl Rubber spatula	Plastic wrap	8½-by-4½-by- 2½-inch loaf pan

1¾ cups (220 grams)
  all-purpose flour
1 cup (115 grams) whole
  wheat flour
1 cup lukewarm water
	2 tablespoons
	  (28 grams) softened
	  butter
	2 tablespoons
	  (42 grams) honey
		1¼ teaspoons salt
		2 teaspoons yeast,
		  instant or active dry
		Nonstick cooking spray

1. **Mix the ingredients.** In a large mixing bowl or the bowl of an electric stand mixer, combine the flours, water, butter, honey, salt, and yeast. Mix until a dough forms that holds together and does not stick to the sides or bottom of the bowl. As the butter melts and is worked into the dough during kneading, it will hydrate the dough, so hold off on adding any more water now even if it seems a bit dry.

2. **Knead the dough.** Knead for 10 to 15 minutes, until it is smooth, soft, and reaches the windowpane stage (meaning that when the dough is stretched, a translucent area appears). If the dough is still dry after 1 to 2 minutes of kneading, sprinkle on water 1 teaspoon at a time. Different brands of whole wheat flour can absorb moisture differently, so the amount of water needed will vary.

3. **The first rise.** Shape the dough gently into a ball and place it inside a clean, lightly oiled bowl. Cover the dough with a clean, damp tea towel and put it in a warm place to rise. Let it rise for 1 hour until it is puffy and has doubled in size.

4. **Shape into a loaf.** Coat the loaf pan with cooking spray. Gently stretch the dough into a rectangle. Use your loaf pan as your guide to make the short side of the rectangle the same length as the longer side of the loaf pan. The rectangle will be about 9 by 18 inches. Tuck in the corners and start to roll in the top of the dough. Roll the dough into a log. Tuck the ends under. Pinch the seams closed, and place the loaf, seam-side down, into the loaf pan.

5. **The second rise.** Cover the dough with heavily greased plastic wrap and put it in a warm place to rise again until it rises to be 1 inch above the top of the loaf pan. The bread will rise very slightly as it bakes, so make sure you are happy with the height of the bread before you bake it. Toward the end of the rising time, preheat your oven to 350°F.

6. **Bake and cool.** Bake for 35 to 40 minutes, until the loaf sounds hollow when tapped. Whole wheat loaves can be difficult to eyeball, because they are naturally darker in color. The finished bread should be between 195°F and 200°F in the center. Remove the bread from the loaf pan, and allow it to cool fully on a wire rack.

7. **Store.** This loaf will stay fresh at room temperature, tightly wrapped, for 3 days. It can be frozen, either whole or sliced, and defrosted in the toaster, in the microwave, or at room temperature. Sliced bread will stay fresh in the freezer for 2 weeks, and a whole frozen loaf will stay fresh for at least 1 month.

DON'T HAVE IT? No whole wheat flour? Just use 100 percent all-purpose flour. Reduce the water to ¾ cup, adding a bit more if needed.

TRY THIS! For extra flair, add up to 3 tablespoons of seeds to the dough. Try pumpkin seeds, poppy seeds, flaxseeds, or 1 tablespoon of each. Add them at the same time as the flour. Keep everything else in the recipe the same. You may want to sprinkle more seeds on top of the loaf just before baking. Brushing the top with water will help the seeds stick.

Buttery Herbed Dinner Rolls

Yield 8 large rolls   Prep 20 minutes   Inactive 2 hours 5 minutes
Bake 20 minutes

The softest, lightest rolls you'll ever try, these dinner rolls are a family favorite. They're fluffy, round, and beautiful. Set them down on the dinner table and watch them disappear.

TOOLS:		
Large mixing bowl	Clean tea towel	Sharp knife
Electric stand mixer	8- or 9-inch-round	Plastic wrap
(optional)	pie pan	
Rubber spatula	Cutting board	

3 cups (450 grams) all-purpose flour	1 tablespoon milk	Nonstick cooking spray
1 cup water	3 tablespoons (36 grams) sugar	2 tablespoons dried Italian seasoning
5 tablespoons (60 grams) softened butter, divided	2 teaspoons yeast, instant or active dry	blend

1. **Mix the ingredients.** In a large mixing bowl or the bowl of an electric stand mixer, combine the flour, water, 2 tablespoons of butter, milk, sugar, and yeast. Mix until a dough is formed that holds together and does not stick to the sides or bottom of the bowl. As the butter melts and is worked into the dough during kneading, it will hydrate the dough, so hold off on adding any more water now, even if it seems a bit dry.

2. **Knead the dough.** Knead for 10 minutes, until the dough is smooth, soft, and reaches the windowpane stage (meaning that when the dough is stretched, a translucent area appears). If the dough is still dry after 1 or 2 minutes of kneading, sprinkle on water 1 teaspoon at a time.

3. **The first rise.** Shape the dough gently into a ball and place it inside a clean, lightly oiled bowl. Cover the dough with a clean, damp tea towel and put it in a warm place to rise. Let it rise for 1 hour or until it is puffy and has doubled in size.

4. **Shape into rolls.** Spray the pan with cooking spray or coat it with butter. Turn the dough out onto a cutting board and gently stretch it into a log. Using a sharp knife, cut the log into eighths. It is easiest to divide it in half, then quarters, and again into eighths. Pick up one ball of dough and pinch the bottom to pull the top of the roll tight. You will see the roll become round and smooth on top as you pinch. Never smash down on the rolls from the top to shape them, or they will be flat and dense. Arrange in the pie plate evenly spaced, pinched-side down. Don't worry about arranging them in any particular order: as they bake, they will form one mass.

5. **The second rise.** Cover the pan with greased plastic wrap and put in a warm place to rise again for about 45 minutes, until the rolls are very puffy and almost cover the bottom of the dish. Toward the end of the rising time, preheat the oven to 375°F. If you put the rolls in the oven to rise, be sure to remove them before preheating.

6. **Brush with the herb-butter mixture.** Melt the remaining 3 tablespoons of butter in a small, microwave-safe bowl and add the Italian seasoning. Mix well, and brush onto the rolls gently. Use all of the butter.

7. **Bake and cool.** Bake for 17 to 20 minutes, or until the rolls are golden brown and 195°F to 200°F in the center. Place the pan on a wire rack to cool for about 20 minutes. Serve right away. (If you can't eat the rolls immediately, be sure to remove them from the dish and let them finish cooling on a rack, otherwise they will get soggy on the bottom.)

Supersoft Italian Bread

Yield 2 loaves Prep 30 minutes Inactive 2 hours 30 minutes
Bake 30 minutes

If my family had to pick a favorite bread recipe, this would be it. The dry powdered milk is a secret ingredient that makes the texture of this bread extra soft and light. You can find it in the baking aisle of your grocery store, usually near canned milk.

TOOLS:		

Large mixing bowl
Rubber spatula
Clean tea towel
Plastic wrap
	Cutting board
	  (optional)
	Baking sheet
	Parchment paper
		Pastry brush or
		  basting brush

3 cups (450 grams)
  all-purpose flour
1 cup water
2 tablespoons
  (26 grams) olive oil
	1 tablespoon dry pow-
	  dered milk
	1¼ teaspoons salt
	1 teaspoon (4 grams)
	  sugar
		2 teaspoons yeast,
		  instant or active dry
		Nonstick cooking spray
		1 egg
		1 tablespoon sesame
		  seeds, divided

1. **Mix the ingredients.** In a large mixing bowl, combine the flour, water, oil, powdered milk, salt, sugar, and yeast. If the mixture is too dry to incorporate all the ingredients, add a bit more water. If the dough is very sticky and won't form a ball, add a bit more flour.

2. **Knead the dough.** Turn the dough out onto a floured surface and knead for 5 to 10 minutes, until the dough feels smooth, stretchy, and elastic. Unless the dough is very sticky, try not to add additional flour to the dough as you knead; you want this dough to be as light as possible. Pick up a golf ball–size piece of dough and try to stretch it flat. If it stretches without immediately tearing, it's ready for the next step. If it tears right away, knead a few more minutes and try again.

3. **The first rise.** Gently shape the dough into a ball and place it inside a clean, lightly oiled bowl. (It can be the same one you mixed the dough in, as long as you wash it out first.) Cover the dough with a damp tea towel or plastic wrap lightly coated with cooking spray. Put the bowl in a warm place, such as a turned-off oven with a bowl of hot water inside. Wait 45 minutes to 1 hour for the first rise, or until the dough has doubled in size.

4. **Roughly shape and rest the loaves.** Turn the dough out onto a clean, lightly floured counter or cutting board. Divide it into two equal pieces. (You can use a scale and measure out two halves if you want them exact.) Gently roll the pieces into 10-inch logs. Cover them with plastic wrap coated in cooking spray and let them rest for 10 minutes on the counter. This will make them easier to stretch out in the next step.

5. **Shape and second rise.** Line a baking sheet with parchment paper or generously coat it with cooking spray. Pull the logs out to be longer and thinner, about 18 inches long. Tuck the ends under and pinch them closed to make the loaves smooth and rounded on the top and side. Place them on the prepared baking sheet about 6 inches apart. In a small bowl, beat the egg for the topping with a fork. Brush it on top of the loaf, covering the top and sides. Sprinkle ½ tablespoon of sesame seeds on each loaf. Cover the dough with greased plastic wrap and put it back into a warm place for the second rise. The second rise will take between 30 and 45 minutes. When the loaves have increased in size noticeably, they are ready to bake. Be careful not to let them over-rise or they will spread out and flatten. Toward the end of the rising time, preheat the oven to 400°F.

6. **Bake and cool.** Remove the plastic wrap, and bake the loaves for 30 minutes. They will be deep golden brown and have an internal temperature of 195°F to 200°F. Because this bread has an egg wash, it will look very deep brown and can look finished on the outside

continued ▶

before it is baked through. If you have an instant-read thermometer, this is a good time to use it to check for doneness. Place the loaves on a wire cooling rack to cool 20 minutes before eating.

EAT IT! These loaves are perfect for slicing and toasting for bruschetta. Slice into ½-inch rounds, brush with olive oil, and broil on a baking sheet for 1 to 2 minutes per side. Let them cool for a few minutes and top with diced tomatoes mixed with olive oil, grated Parmesan, and fresh basil.

DON'T HAVE IT? Don't want to use the powdered milk? Add ¼ cup of regular milk, and reduce the water to ¾ of a cup.

Simple Slider Buns for Burgers

Yield 16 small slider rolls   Prep 20 minutes   Inactive 2 hours
30 minutes   Bake 16 minutes

There's something about a slider that's more exciting than a burger, isn't there? This recipe makes perfectly sized buns that will take any sandwich recipe to the next level. As a bonus, they freeze perfectly, meaning you can defrost one and have a little snack-size sandwich whenever you want.

TOOLS:		
Large mixing bowl	Rubber spatula	2 baking sheets
Electric stand mixer	Clean tea towel	Sharp knife
(optional)	Plastic wrap	Cutting board

3 cups (375 grams)
  flour
¾ cup milk
2 tablespoons
  (28 grams) softened
  butter

3 tablespoons water
1 tablespoon
  (12 grams) sugar
2 eggs, divided

2 teaspoons yeast,
  instant or active dry
2 tablespoons sesame
  seeds or poppy seeds

1. **Mix the ingredients.** In a large mixing bowl or the bowl of an electric stand mixer, combine the flour, milk, butter, water, sugar, eggs, and yeast. Mix until a dough is formed that holds together and does not stick to the sides or bottom of the bowl. As the butter melts, it will hydrate the dough during kneading, so hold off on adding any more water now even if it seems a bit dry. The dough should be smooth, golden in color, and slightly sticky.

2. **Knead the dough.** Knead for 10 minutes, until the dough is smooth, soft, and reaches the windowpane stage (meaning that when the dough is stretched, a translucent area appears). As you knead, any stickiness should go away, and the dough should feel smooth and bouncy under your hands.

continued ▶

3. **The first rise.** Shape the dough gently into a ball and place it inside a clean, lightly oiled bowl. (It can be the same one you mixed the dough in, as long as you wash it out first.) Cover the dough with a clean, damp tea towel or plastic wrap and put it in a warm place to rise. Let it rise for 1 hour, or until it is puffy and has doubled in size. This is an enriched dough (meaning it contains butter, milk, sugar, and eggs), so it rises a bit slower than other doughs.

4. **Shape into rolls.** Line the two baking sheets with parchment paper. Remove the dough from the bowl, and gently stretch it into a log. Using a sharp knife and a cutting board, cut the log into 16 equal pieces. It is easiest to divide the log in half, then quarters, and twice more until you have 16 pieces of dough. Gently shape the dough pieces into smooth balls by pinching the bottoms. Place them on the parchment-paper-lined baking sheets about 2 inches apart. Then slightly flatten them, using your fingertips. Don't squish them flat, just press them into disks.

5. **The second rise.** Cover the buns with heavily greased plastic wrap and put them in a warm place to rise again for 25 to 30 minutes, until they are puffy but not doubled in size. In a small bowl, beat the egg for the topping with a fork, and brush it on top of the buns. Sprinkle sesame seeds or poppy seeds on top. Toward the end of the rising time, preheat your oven to 400°F.

6. **Bake.** Bake the buns for 14 to 16 minutes, making sure to switch the baking sheets halfway through the baking time. The baking time on these is short, so you could also bake them one sheet at a time without worrying about the second batch over-rising. They are done when they are deep golden brown and the internal temperature is 190°F. Because they have an egg wash, they will be quite browned before they are baked through. When the rolls are done, let them cool on a wire rack. If you are slicing them for burgers, let them cool for at least 45 minutes, or until completely cool.

KNEAD HELP? This is a stickier dough than some you might have worked with. If you're finding it difficult to knead or shape, try spraying your hands with some cooking spray. It's a better choice than adding flour, which will make your finished buns too dense.

EAT IT! Would you believe that leftover homemade burger buns make the best bread pudding? Strange, but true: they are soft but still hold their shape. To make bread pudding, cut up the buns until you have 6 cups of cubed bread. Mix up 2 cups of milk, ¼ cup of melted butter, 2 eggs, ½ cup of sugar, and 1 teaspoon of cinnamon. Place the bread cubes in a 9-by-13-inch casserole dish, pour the milk mixture on top, and bake for 40 minutes at 350°F.

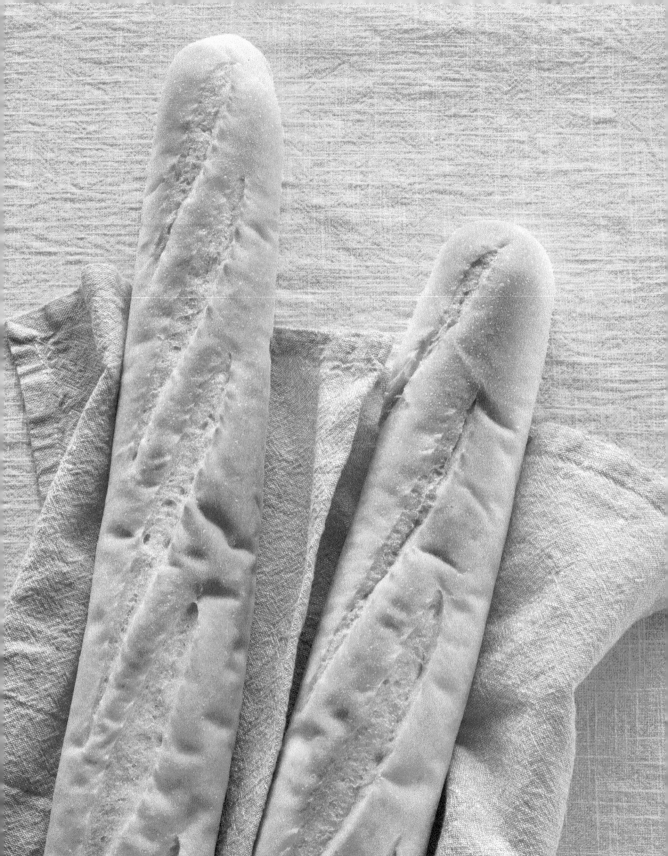

Simple French Baguettes with a Crisp Crust

Yield 2 medium baguettes   Prep 20 minutes   Inactive 8 hours
Bake 20 minutes

Traditional baguettes are made with a poolish and take at least a day to make. This recipe simplifies things. These baguettes are faster and easier but still have a crisp crust and lots of chewiness yet are ready in one day. The rising times are a bit longer than you might be used to, so start these in the morning to have them ready for dinner. They are a great hands-off recipe: think of them as "low-knead"!

TOOLS:		
Large mixing bowl Rubber spatula Clean tea towel Plastic wrap	Sharp knife or bench scraper Parchment paper	2 baking sheets (at least one must be rimmed) Lame (optional)

3 cups (390 grams)
  bread flour
1 cup water
½ teaspoon (2 grams)
  sugar

1½ teaspoons salt
1 teaspoon yeast,
  instant or active dry

Cornmeal, to line
  baking sheet
  (optional)

1. **Combine the ingredients in a large bowl.** In a large mixing bowl, combine the bread flour, water, sugar, salt, and yeast. This dough will look slightly dry, but it should still form a ball. If it's too dry, slowly add water and stir until it forms a ball. Cover and allow to rest at room temperature for about 30 minutes.

2. **Knead the dough.** Check the consistency of the dough, and add a tiny bit of water or flour until the dough is soft but not wet or sticky. You don't want this dough to be too hydrated, or the baguettes will not hold their shape as they rise. Turn the dough out onto the

continued ▶

counter. It should be smooth and easy to work with and not sticky at all. Knead for 2 minutes. The consistency will not change very much because this is such a short kneading time. Don't worry about checking how stretchy the dough is.

3. **The first rise.** Gently shape the dough into a ball and place it in a clean and lightly oiled mixing bowl. (It can be the same one you mixed the dough in, as long as you wash it out first.) Cover the dough with a damp tea towel or greased plastic wrap. Let it rise on the counter for 4 to 6 hours, until it's doubled in size. The warmer your room, the less time it will take to rise. If you've covered the bowl with a damp tea towel, check it from time to time and remoisten it if it starts to dry out.

4. **Rest the dough and shape it into baguettes.** Turn the dough out onto the counter, and divide it in half using a knife or bench scraper, if you have one. Shape the dough into 2 roughly 10- to 12-inch logs by simply stretching them out. Cover the dough with a damp, clean towel and let the logs rest for 15 minutes. This will make them easier to shape. Line a baking sheet with parchment paper or very generously sprinkle it with cornmeal. Shape the baguettes by rolling each piece out until it is 15 inches long. Place them both on the prepared baking sheet at least 6 inches apart. There is no need to tuck the ends under or shape them in any way. Rub the baguettes generously with flour, and make five slashes on the top using a sharp knife or lame.

5. **The second rise.** Cover the dough with greased plastic wrap. Let it rise in a warm place, such as a slightly warm but turned-off oven, for 1 hour. The baguettes should be very puffy before baking.

6. **Bake and cool.** Arrange your oven racks so that one rack is in the center and one rack is in the lowest position. Place a rimmed baking sheet on the lower rack. Pour 2 cups of water into the rimmed baking sheet. This will create a gentle steam effect that will help the

baguettes have a crisper crust. Preheat the oven to 425°F. Once the oven has preheated, place the baguettes on the center rack and bake for 20 minutes. When they are finished, they will be light golden brown and 200°F in the center. Remove them from the oven and place them on a wire cooling rack. (Wait until the rimmed baking sheet is completely cool before removing it to avoid burning yourself with hot water!). Allow the baguettes to cool for 30 minutes before serving. Serve sliced into rounds with appetizers such as bruschetta or dips or slice them horizontally and make a sandwich.

Brown Sugar and Oatmeal Sandwich Bread

Yield 1 loaf Prep 20 minutes Inactive 3 hours Bake 40 minutes

With just enough butter and sugar to make it extra soft and a little sweet, this is the perfect bread for a good old-fashioned PB&J.

TOOLS:		
Large mixing bowl Rubber spatula	Cutting board (optional) Plastic wrap	8½-by-4½-by-2½-inch loaf pan Pastry brush

1¼ cup boiling water ¼ cup (54 grams) softened butter ½ cup old-fashioned oats, plus extra for decorating the top of the loaf	¼ cup (49 grams) brown sugar 1½ teaspoons salt 2¼ cups (282 grams) all-purpose flour	½ cup (57 grams) whole wheat flour 2 teaspoons yeast, instant or active dry Nonstick cooking spray

1. **Mix the oats and cool.** In a large mixing bowl, combine the boiling water, butter, and oats, and mix well. Let the bowl rest on the counter until it is warm but not hot. To ensure you don't kill the yeast, don't rush this step. It should be under 100°F before moving on to the next step.

2. **Add the remaining ingredients to form a dough.** Add the brown sugar, salt, all-purpose flour, whole wheat flour, and yeast. Stir well to form a loose ball of dough. If the dough appears dry and crumbly, slowly add more water and stir until a dough forms. If it seems too wet and is sticking to the bowl, add flour slowly until it forms a ball.

3. **Knead.** Turn the dough out onto a clean, lightly floured countertop or cutting board. Knead for 10 minutes, until the dough is smooth and feels stretchy and elastic. Whole wheat flour and oatmeal are slower

to develop gluten, which is why this dough needs a little more kneading time than some other recipes. When you can stretch the dough a few inches without it tearing, it's time to move on to the rising phase.

4. **The first rise.** Lightly oil a large, clean mixing bowl with cooking spray. (It can be the same one you mixed the dough in, as long as you wash it out first.) Gently shape the dough into a ball and place it inside the bowl. Cover the dough with a damp tea towel or lightly greased plastic wrap and put it in a warm place to rise for 1 hour. It may take a bit longer due to the oatmeal and whole wheat flour in the recipe. When the dough has doubled in size, it's ready to shape.

5. **Shape into a loaf.** Coat the loaf pan with cooking spray. Gently stretch the dough into a rectangle. Use your loaf pan as your guide to make the short side of the rectangle the same length as the longer side of the loaf pan. The rectangle will be about 9 by 18 inches. Tuck in the corners and start to roll in the top of the dough. Roll the dough into a log. Tuck the ends under. Pinch the seams closed, and place the loaf, seam-side down, into the loaf pan.

6. **The second rise.** Cover the dough with greased plastic wrap and set it in a warm place to rise until the loaf is 2 inches over the top of the pan, about 45 minutes. Again, the oatmeal will slightly slow down the rising process. Toward the end of the rising time, preheat your oven to 350°F with the rack in the center.

7. **Bake and cool.** If you'd like to decorate the top of the bread, brush it gently with water and press whole oats on top. Be careful not to squash down the dough. Bake for 35 to 45 minutes, or until golden brown on top and between 195°F and 205°F. Cool on a wire rack for 1 hour, if slicing for sandwiches. Allow the bread to cool completely before slicing. It will stay fresh at room temperature, tightly wrapped, for 3 days, or frozen up to 1 month.

Extra-Soft Garlic Breadsticks

Yield 24 small breadsticks **Prep** 20 minutes **Inactive** 2 hours
Bake 16 minutes

These breadsticks are soft, a little salty, and very addictive. I always make them small so that everyone can keep asking for more without filling up too much. If you are having guests over for dinner and want to make something that's a guaranteed success, make this recipe!

TOOLS:		
Large mixing bowl Rubber spatula Clean tea towel Plastic wrap	2 baking sheets Parchment paper Cutting board Sharp knife	Small microwave-safe bowl Pastry brush

For the dough

3 cups (390 grams)
bread flour
1 cup water
3 tablespoons
(42 grams) butter,
softened
1½ teaspoons salt

1 tablespoon
(12 grams) granulated
sugar
2 teaspoons active dry
or instant yeast

For the topping

2 tablespoons
(28 grams) melted
butter
½ teaspoon garlic salt
1 teaspoon chopped
fresh parsley
(optional)

1. **Mix the ingredients.** In a large mixing bowl, combine the flour, water, butter, salt, sugar, and yeast. Mix until a dough is formed that holds together and does not stick to the sides or bottom of the bowl. As the butter melts and is worked into the dough during kneading, it will make the dough smoother.

2. **Knead the dough.** Knead for 5 to 10 minutes, until the dough is smooth, soft, and reaches the windowpane stage (meaning that when the dough is stretched, a translucent area appears). As you knead, any sticky feeling should go away and the dough should feel smooth, soft, and elastic.

continued ▶

3. The first rise. Shape the dough gently into a ball and place it inside a clean, lightly oiled bowl. (It can be the same one you mixed the dough in, as long as you wash it out first.) Cover the dough with a clean, damp tea towel or plastic wrap and put in a warm place to rise. Let it rise for 1 hour or until it is puffy and has doubled in size. The dough is light and should rise relatively quickly.

4. Shape into breadsticks. Line the two baking sheets with parchment paper. Turn out the dough onto a cutting board and gently stretch it into a log. Cut the log into 24 equal pieces. It is easiest to divide it in half, then quarters, then eighths. Finally, divide each eighth into 3 pieces so you have a total of 24 pieces. (If you would like to make sure each breadstick is exactly the same size, use a digital scale. Weigh the total weight of the dough in grams, divide by 24, and then portion out pieces of dough by weight.) Gently shape the dough pieces into smooth logs, gently stretching them out to be 4 inches long. Cover them lightly with a damp towel or greased plastic wrap, and let them rest on the counter for 10 minutes to make them easier to shape. After the rest period, roll them out into 6-inch smooth logs. Place them on the parchment-paper-lined baking sheets about 2 inches apart.

5. The second rise. Cover the trays with heavily greased plastic wrap, and put them in a warm place to rise again for 25 to 30 minutes, until the breadsticks are puffy but not doubled in size. They will rise quickly because they are so small, so keep an eye on them. Toward the end of the rising time, preheat your oven to 350°F.

6. Bake and top. Bake for 14 to 16 minutes, switching the baking sheets halfway through the bake time. While they are baking, prepare the topping. Melt the butter in a small microwave-safe bowl and measure out the garlic salt. When the breadsticks are finished baking, you should be ready to immediately add the topping while they are still hot. The breadsticks will not look very brown when they are done; this is okay. It's important not to overbake because you want them

to be very soft. They are done when they are light golden brown and the internal temperature is around 195°F. Remove the baking sheets, and immediately brush the breadsticks with the melted butter and sprinkle with the garlic salt and the parsley, if using. Let them finish cooling on a wire cooling rack for about 15 minutes, until cool enough to handle. Eat immediately.

TRY THIS! For an Italian-inspired flavor, add 2 teaspoons of dried herbs (basil, oregano, or an Italian seasoning blend) into the dough during step 1. As soon as the breadsticks come out of the oven, sprinkle grated Parmesan cheese on top along with the garlic salt.

KNEAD HELP? Having trouble shaping the breadsticks? They will look a little bit lumpy on the ends at first, but as they rise and bake, they will smooth out. Don't worry about making them look perfect during the shaping process!

5

SWEET BREADS

Baking sweet breads opens up a new world for you. Bread is no longer just for sandwiches and served with dinner but can be a lovely breakfast, an afternoon snack, or dessert. Keep in mind that these recipes are a bit slower to rise because they have sugar and, in most cases, milk and butter. They are still easy to make, so don't worry. You're sure to find a few favorites in this collection of sweet treats. Have fun with these recipes.

Chocolate Chip Brioche Loaf

Yield 1 loaf Prep 20 minutes Inactive 3 hours Bake 40 minutes

If you're looking for a beautiful presentation, this is your recipe. It's deep golden brown, glossy, and studded with chocolate. No one can resist. This is a wintertime staple at our house, always served with hot chocolate. Not only is it warm, sweet, and cozy, but it's much easier to make in a cooler house.

TOOLS:		
Mixing bowl, one large and one small Rubber spatula	Electric stand mixer (optional) 8½-by-4½-by-2½-inch loaf pan	Plastic wrap Fork Pastry brush

¼ cup water	3 tablespoons (36 grams) sugar	Nonstick cooking spray
¼ cup milk	3 cups (375 grams) all-purpose flour	1¼ cups chocolate chips or chocolate chunks
3 tablespoons (42 grams) butter, softened	1 teaspoon salt	Coarse sugar, for topping
4 eggs, divided	2 teaspoons yeast, instant or active dry	

1. **Mix the ingredients.** Combine the water, milk, butter, 3 eggs, sugar, flour, salt, and yeast in a large mixing bowl. Mix well with a spatula to make sure everything is incorporated. As the butter softens, it will hydrate the dough even more. The dough will be very soft and somewhat sticky.

2. **Knead.** If you have an electric stand mixer, it will come in handy for this recipe, so you don't have to handle the sticky dough. If you don't, just knead by hand! Fit the stand mixer with the hook attachment, transfer the dough into the bowl, and let the machine run on low for 5 to 7 minutes. To knead by hand, turn the dough out onto a lightly floured surface. Spray your hands with nonstick cooking spray and

rub them together. Knead for 7 to 10 minutes. You will find that as you knead, the dough becomes less sticky.

3. **Add the chocolate chips.** When the dough is smooth, soft, and easy to handle, add the chocolate chips. Knead very gently until they are just combined. If your kitchen or hands are very warm, the chocolate chips may melt a little bit. This is fine; just try to handle them as little as possible. When the chocolate chips are worked into the dough, gently shape it into a ball.

4. **The first rise.** Lightly coat a large, clean mixing bowl with cooking spray. Place the dough inside and cover it with greased plastic wrap. Tuck the bowl in a warm place, such as a warmed but turned-off oven, for 1 hour to 1 hour, 30 minutes. The dough is ready when it is very puffy and has doubled in size. Because this is an enriched dough that contains eggs, milk, butter, and sugar, it is slower to rise than other doughs.

5. **Shape into a loaf.** Turn the dough out onto a clean counter. Using the long edge of the loaf pan as your guide, stretch the dough out into a 9-by-18-inch rectangle. Handle the dough lightly to avoid getting melted chocolate all over the loaf or yourself. (If it does streak, don't worry. It will bake perfectly fine.) Tuck in the top two corners, tuck down the top edge, and roll down into a log. Tuck the ends under and pinch all the seams shut. Coat the loaf pan with cooking spray and gently place the loaf inside, seam-side down.

6. **The second rise.** Cover the dough with greased plastic wrap, and store the loaf back in a warm place to rise again until the dough rises 1½ inches over the top edge of the loaf pan. This will take between 45 minutes and 1 hour. Toward the end of the rising time, preheat the oven to 400°F with a rack in the center.

7. **Top with egg wash and coarse sugar.** In a small mixing bowl, beat 1 egg for the topping with a fork until thoroughly mixed. Brush it on

continued ▶

top of the loaf and sprinkle it with coarse sugar. (Regular granulated sugar will work as well.)

8. Bake. Bake the brioche for 35 to 40 minutes, or until it is deep golden brown and has reached an internal temperature of 195°F. Like any bread with an egg wash, it will look quite dark as it bakes. Don't be tempted to take it out of the oven too soon because it is browning quickly.

9. Cool and slice. Carefully remove the bread from the loaf pan and place it on a wire rack to cool. If chocolate chips have melted onto the edge of the pan, run a butter knife along the outside of the loaf to make it easier to remove. Cool for at least 20 minutes before serving.

Apple Pie Bread

Yield 1 loaf Prep 20 minutes Inactive 2 hours 15 minutes Bake 30 minutes

For a memorable holiday breakfast, you'll turn to this recipe over and over. Canned apple pie filling is convenient and delicious. There's hardly any shaping required, and the glaze takes seconds to mix up. This is one of the very easiest breads you can make.

TOOLS:		
Mixing bowls, one large and one small Rubber spatula	Plastic wrap 9-by-13-inch baking dish	Sharp knife Small whisk

3 cups (375 grams) all-purpose flour	5½ tablespoons milk, divided	2 teaspoons yeast
¾ cup water	2 tablespoons (25 grams) granulated sugar	1 (21-ounce) can apple pie filling
3 tablespoons (43 grams) butter, room temperature	1 teaspoon salt	2 cups (241 grams) powdered sugar

1. **Mix the ingredients.** In a large mixing bowl, combine the flour, water, butter, 3 tablespoons of milk, the granulated sugar, the salt, and the yeast and mix well to incorporate everything. If the dough seems too dry and crumbly, add more milk 1 teaspoon at a time. The butter, as it melts, will add moisture to the dough, so don't worry if it looks slightly dry at first.

2. **Knead the dough.** Turn the dough out onto a clean countertop, and knead for 5 to 7 minutes. The dough should not be too sticky to knead by hand, but if it is, sprinkle a small amount of flour until it is smooth, soft, and easy to handle. Knead until the dough feels stretchy and elastic.

continued ▶

3. *The first rise.* Place the dough inside a clean, lightly oiled bowl and cover it with greased plastic wrap. Put the bowl in a warm place, such as a warmed but turned-off oven. Let the dough rise until it has doubled in size and is very puffy. This will take about 1 hour, or maybe a few minutes more, because this dough contains butter, sugar, and milk.

4. *Divide and shape the dough.* Coat a 9-by-13-inch baking dish with cooking spray. Cut the dough in half with a sharp knife. Take one half of the dough and stretch it to cover the bottom of the baking dish. If it pulls back and seems hard to stretch out, let it rest covered for 10 minutes, then come back and try again. Try to stretch the dough out to completely cover the dish.

5. *Add the filling and more dough.* Pour the can of apple pie filling on top of the dough and spread it out evenly from edge to edge so that it completely covers the dough. Stretch out the second half of the dough into a rough rectangle on the counter, then lift it up and place it on top of the pie filling. Stretch it out a bit more to cover as much of the pie filling as possible.

6. *The second rise.* Cover the dish with greased plastic wrap and put it in a warm place to rise. Allow the dough to rise for 45 minutes to 1 hour, until it is very puffy and has risen almost to the top of the baking dish. Toward the end of the rising time, preheat your oven to 350°F with the rack in the center.

7. *Bake.* Bake the bread for 25 to 30 minutes, until light golden brown on the top and baked through. It's ready when the bottom layer of dough reaches 200°F. Cool for 15 minutes on a heatproof surface while you make the glaze.

8. **Make the glaze.** In a small mixing bowl, whisk together the powdered sugar with the remaining 2 tablespoons of milk to make the glaze. It should be pourable but still thick. If it's too thick and is more of a solid, add the additional ½ tablespoon of milk.

9. **Glaze and serve.** After 15 minutes, pour the glaze evenly on top, using all of it. When the glaze has hardened, cut the bread into squares and serve. Refrigerate any leftovers.

TRY THIS! You can add any pie filling to the center of this recipe. Cherry and blackberry are also delicious. Be sure to check the size of the can. (Anything more than 22 ounces will be too much and will weigh down the dough.)

Soft Cinnamon Rolls with Cream Cheese Frosting

Yield 16 rolls **Prep** 25 minutes **Inactive** 2 hours **Bake** 30 minutes

Cinnamon rolls are a treat for breakfast, but who wants to wake up before dawn to start them? Go ahead and make and shape them before bed and pop them in the refrigerator, covered. In the morning, you'll just need to let them finish rising and bake. What a great way to start the day.

TOOLS:		

Large mixing bowl
Rubber spatula
Cutting board
  (optional)
Clean tea towel
	Plastic wrap
	Medium
	  microwave-safe
	  bowl
	Rolling pin
		Sharp knife
		9-by-13-inch baking
		  dish
		Electric mixer (for the
		  frosting)

For the dough
2¾ cups (344 grams)
  all-purpose flour
¼ cup milk
¼ cup plus
  1 tablespoon water
4 tablespoons
  (57 grams) butter
¼ cup (50 grams)
  granulated sugar
2 teaspoons yeast,
  instant or active dry

1 egg
1 teaspoon vanilla
¾ teaspoon salt

For the filling
½ cup (113 grams)
  butter, unsalted
¼ cup (50 grams)
  sugar
2 tablespoons
  cinnamon
Pinch salt

For the cream cheese frosting
3 ounces cream
  cheese, softened
3 tablespoons
  (43 grams) butter,
  softened
3 cups (363 grams)
  powdered sugar
2 tablespoons milk
1 teaspoon vanilla
  extract
¼ teaspoon salt

1. **Mix the ingredients.** In a large mixing bowl, use a spatula to combine the flour, milk, ¼ cup of water, butter, granulated sugar, yeast, egg, vanilla, and salt. Make sure all the ingredients are well incorporated. If there are dry bits of flour, add 1 more tablespoon of water until the dough comes together.

2. **Knead the dough.** Turn the dough out onto a clean counter or cutting board. Knead for 10 minutes, or until the dough is soft, smooth, and stretchy. When you start kneading and the butter works through the dough, it might seem wet and sticky. As you keep kneading, it should become less sticky. If it is difficult to work with, lightly flour the counter and your hands to prevent sticking. Adding too much flour will make the rolls dense. When the dough feels elastic and smooth, it is ready for the first rise.

3. **The first rise.** Gently shape the dough into a loose ball. Place the dough inside a clean, lightly oiled bowl and cover it with a clean, damp tea towel or plastic wrap. Let it rise in a warm place for 1 hour, until it has doubled in size and is very puffy. This enriched dough may take longer to rise, so give it more time if necessary.

4. **Make the filling.** Melt the butter in the microwave on low for 30 seconds in a medium-size microwave-safe bowl. Add the sugar, cinnamon, and salt, and mix until everything is thoroughly combined. Spread 1 tablespoon of the filling mixture on the bottom of the baking dish. This will prevent the rolls from sticking and add a little flavor to the outside of the buns.

5. **Roll and fill.** Lightly flour a clean countertop and turn the dough onto the counter. Using a rolling pin, flatten the dough into a 10-by-16-inch rectangle. (If you don't want to measure the rectangle, just use your baking dish as a guide and shape a slightly bigger rectangle.) Spread the remaining filling mixture evenly across the dough, leaving a 1-inch border on all sides. Carefully roll the rectangle from bottom to top into a rope shape. There will be one long seam; be sure to pinch it shut.

6. **Slice and arrange.** Cut the rope into 1-inch pieces with a very sharp knife (a large, serrated bread knife works well). You should have 16 portions. (If not, that's okay! A few more or less is fine.) Place each

continued ▶

piece in the baking dish so that it lies flat and the swirl pattern is visible.

7. **The second rise.** Cover the dish with greased plastic wrap and tuck it in a warm place to rise again. (If you're prepping this to bake later, this is the time to put it in the refrigerator.) The second rise will take between 45 minutes and 1 hour. The rolls are ready to bake when they have almost doubled in size and are touching or nearly touching each other on the sides. Toward the end of the rising time, preheat your oven to 350°F with the rack in the center.

8. **Bake and cool.** Bake the cinnamon rolls for 25 to 30 minutes, until golden brown on the top. Place the baking dish on a heatproof surface to cool while you make the cream cheese frosting.

9. **Make the frosting.** Combine the cream cheese, butter, and powdered sugar using an electric mixer. Start mixing on low, then increase the speed to medium-high once the sugar is mixed in. Add the milk, vanilla, and salt. Beat for 2 to 3 minutes, or until smooth, and spread the frosting on top of the still-warm cinnamon buns. Serve immediately. Any leftovers will keep in the refrigerator, tightly covered, for up to 5 days.

Pineapple Coconut Sweet Rolls

Yield 16 rolls Prep 20 minutes Inactive 2 hours 45 minutes
Bake 30 minutes

The perfect sweet bread for when you need a vacation. My family and I first tried rolls like this at a Hawaiian buffet. I spent the rest of the week trying to figure out how to copy them. As soon as we came home, I got to work on this recipe for sweet, tropical rolls that taste like a dessert but can pass as a breakfast.

TOOLS:		

Large mixing bowl
Rubber spatula
Cutting board
  (optional)
Clean tea towel
	Plastic wrap
	Rolling pin
	9-by-13-inch baking
	  dish
		Sharp knife
		Electric mixer for the
		  frosting

For the dough

2¾ cups (344 grams)
  all-purpose flour

¼ cup milk

¼ cup plus
  1 tablespoon water

4 tablespoons
  (57 grams) butter

¼ cup (50 grams)
  granulated sugar

2 teaspoons yeast,
  instant or active dry

1 egg

1 teaspoon vanilla
  extract

¾ teaspoon salt

For the filling

1 (12-ounce) jar pre-
  pared pineapple
  preserves

**For the icing
and topping**

1¼ cups (150 grams)
  powdered sugar

4 tablespoons
  (56 grams) unsalted
  butter, melted

½ teaspoon vanilla
  extract

Pinch salt

3 tablespoons milk

1 cup sweetened shred-
  ded coconut

1. **Mix the ingredients.** In a large mixing bowl, use a spatula to combine the flour, milk, ¼ cup of water, and the butter, granulated sugar, yeast, egg, vanilla, and salt. Make sure all the ingredients are well

incorporated. If there are dry bits of flour, add 1 more tablespoon of water until the dough comes together.

2. **Knead the dough.** Turn the dough out onto a clean counter or cutting board. Knead for 10 minutes, or until the dough is soft, smooth, and stretchy. As you knead, the dough will firm up and feel less sticky. If it is very difficult to work with, lightly flour the counter and your hands to prevent sticking. Or spray your hands with cooking spray and rub them together. Avoid adding too much flour, because this will make the rolls dense. Knead until the dough feels smooth and elastic.

3. **The first rise.** Gently shape the dough into a loose ball. Place the dough inside a clean, lightly oiled bowl and cover it with a clean, damp tea towel or with plastic wrap. Let it rise in a warm place for 1 hour to 1 hour, 30 minutes, or until it has doubled in size and is very puffy.

4. **Shape and the add filling.** Turn the dough out onto the lightly floured counter. Using a rolling pin, flatten the dough into a 10-by-15-inch rectangle. Spread the pineapple preserves evenly across the dough. Leave a 1-inch border on all sides. Carefully roll the longer side of the rectangle into a rope shape. Be sure to pinch the long seam shut.

5. **Slice and arrange.** Coat the baking dish in cooking spray. Cut the rope into 1-inch slices with a very sharp knife (a large, serrated bread knife works well). Some of the pineapple preserves may leak out; this is okay. The sharper the knife, the less leakage there will be. Arrange the slices, equally spaced, in the baking dish.

6. **The second rise.** Cover the dish with greased plastic wrap and put it in a warm place to rise again. The second rise will take between 45 minutes and 1 hour. The rolls will have almost doubled in size and be touching or nearly touching each other on the sides. Toward the end of the rising time, preheat your oven to 350°F with the rack in the center.

continued ▶

7. **Bake.** Bake the pineapple rolls for 25 to 30 minutes, until golden brown on the top. The areas where the preserves have leaked will become very browned due to the sugar in the filling. This is normal, and the icing will cover it up, so don't worry. Cool the baking dish on a heatproof surface while you prepare the frosting.

8. **Make the icing and add the coconut.** In a large mixing bowl, combine the powdered sugar and melted butter, beating until smooth with an electric mixer. Add the vanilla, salt, and milk, and beat for 1 minute. Pour the icing on top of the pineapple rolls and spread it out with a spatula. Sprinkle the coconut on top while the frosting is still wet. Allow the icing to set for 15 minutes before serving. Refrigerate any leftovers and eat within 5 days.

DON'T HAVE IT? If you can't find pineapple preserves, you can make your own pineapple filling. You'll need a 15-ounce can of crushed pineapple (undrained) and ¼ cup of sugar. Combine them in a medium saucepan, bring to a boil over medium-high heat, then reduce to a simmer. Let the mixture bubble for about 10 minutes, until it slightly thickens.

Classic Braided Challah

Yield 1 loaf Prep 20 minutes Inactive 3 hours 5 minutes Bake 30 minutes

Challah is traditionally made with a six-strand braid that is tricky to master. This recipe uses the same rich, slightly sweet dough but is made with only a three-strand braid that is much easier to work with. This loaf comes out of the oven looking shiny, golden, and beautiful.

TOOLS:		
Mixing bowl, one large and one small Rubber spatula	Clean tea towel Plastic wrap Baking sheet	Parchment paper Fork or whisk Pastry brush

4 cups (500 grams) all-purpose flour	¼ cup (50 grams) sugar	1½ teaspoons salt
¾ cup plus 1 tablespoon water	¼ cup (56 grams) melted butter	1 egg
2½ teaspoons yeast, instant or active dry	2 eggs	3 tablespoons sesame seeds

1. **Mix the ingredients.** In a large mixing bowl, combine the flour, water, yeast, sugar, butter, eggs, and salt using a spatula. Make sure all the ingredients are well incorporated. If there are dry bits of flour, add 1 more tablespoon of water until the dough comes together.

2. **Knead the dough.** Turn the dough out onto a clean counter or cutting board. Knead for 10 minutes, or until the dough is soft, smooth, and stretchy. The dough will firm up as you knead and feel less sticky as you work with it. If it is very difficult to work with, lightly flour the counter and your hands to prevent sticking.

3. **The first rise.** Gently shape the dough into a loose ball. Place the dough inside a clean, lightly oiled bowl and cover it with a clean, damp tea towel or with plastic wrap. Let it rise in a warm place for 1 hour to 1 hour, 30 minutes, or until it has doubled in size and is very puffy.

continued ▶

4. **Divide and rest.** Turn the dough out onto a clean counter and divide it in thirds. Dividing into thirds can be hard to eyeball, so if you'd like the pieces to be perfectly even, weigh your dough in grams, divide by three, and portion each piece to that weight. Stretch them into 10-inch logs, cover them with a damp tea towel, and let them rest on the counter for 30 minutes.

5. **Stretch into longer ropes and braid.** Roll out each rope between your palms until it is 16 inches long. Line a baking sheet with parchment paper. Place the three ropes on the parchment paper and pinch the tops together. Braid the loaf by crossing the rope on the right over the center, then the rope on the left over the center, and so on, continuing until the loaf is braided. Pinch the bottom of the braid closed and tuck both ends under.

6. **Add toppings.** Beat the egg for the topping in a small bowl using a fork or small whisk. Brush it over the loaf using a pastry brush. Sprinkle sesame seeds on top, and gently press them on to help them stick.

7. **The second rise.** Coat some plastic wrap with cooking spray and gently drape it over the dough. Place the loaf in a warm place to rise again for 30 to 45 minutes. Don't let the loaf over-rise, or the braid pattern will be ruined. Halfway through the rising time, preheat your oven to 375°F with the rack in the center.

8. **Bake and cool.** Bake for 30 minutes, until the top is very golden brown and the bread has an internal temperature of 195°F. Allow the bread to cool on a wire rack for at least 20 minutes before serving.

Lemon Sugar Sweet Rolls

Yield 16 rolls Prep 25 minutes Inactive 2 hours 35 minutes
Bake 20 minutes

If you like crunchy sugar (and who doesn't?), you will love the combination of sugar and fresh lemon zest in these rolls. These probably make the most sense as a breakfast, but I have served them as a dinner roll, and no one has complained! You'll use lemon zest for this recipe but not the juice, so have a recipe in mind for later to use the juice.

TOOLS:		

Large mixing bowl
Rubber spatula
Plastic wrap
	Sharp knife
	Baking sheet
	Parchment paper
		2 small bowls (one
		  should be micro-
		  waveable)

For the dough

¼ cup milk

¼ cup water

3 tablespoons
(43 grams) unsalted
butter, softened

¼ cup
(50 grams) white
sugar

**2 cups (250 grams)
all-purpose flour**

1 teaspoon salt

**1½ teaspoons yeast,
instant or active dry**

**1 teaspoon grated
lemon zest**

**For the lemon
sugar topping**

**¼ cup (56 grams)
butter**

**½ cup
(100 grams) white
sugar**

**2 tablespoons grated
lemon zest**

1. **Combine the dough ingredients.** Combine the milk, water, softened butter, sugar, flour, salt, yeast, and 1 teaspoon of lemon zest in a large mixing bowl. The dough will be slightly sticky and will stick to the spatula and sides of the bowl as you mix.

2. **Knead the dough.** Turn the dough out onto a clean, lightly floured countertop and knead for 7 to 10 minutes. As you knead, the dough will become less sticky. Try to avoid adding more flour right away; knead for a few minutes first. If the dough is too difficult to knead,

continued ▶

add 1 tablespoon of flour. Continue to knead until the dough feels soft, smooth, and elastic.

3. **The first rise.** Gently shape the dough into a ball and place it in a large, lightly oiled mixing bowl. Cover the dough with a damp tea towel or plastic wrap and allow it to rise in a warm place for 1 hour to 1 hour, 30 minutes, or until it is doubled in size and very puffy. Because this is an enriched dough, it may take a little extra time.

4. **Divide the dough.** Turn out the dough onto a clean countertop. Divide into 16 roughly equal pieces using a sharp knife. It is easiest to divide the dough in half, then quarters, etc. If you want the rolls to be exactly the same size, weigh your total dough in grams, divide by 16, and portion out the dough to match $\frac{1}{16}$ of the total weight.

5. **Shape into rolls.** Line a baking sheet with parchment paper. Pick up one portion of dough, and pinch the bottom to pull the top tight. You will see the roll become round and smooth on top as you pinch. Never smash down on the rolls from the top to shape them, or they will be flat and dense. Place the rolls on the parchment paper at least 3 inches apart.

6. **The second rise.** Cover the baking sheet with heavily greased plastic wrap, and put the rolls in a warm place to rise again. Rolls rise faster than a loaf of bread, so keep an eye on them. They will take 30 to 45 minutes. The rolls will not double in size but will become puffy. Halfway through the rising time, preheat your oven to 350°F with a rack in the center.

7. **Make the topping.** Melt ¼ cup of butter in a microwave-safe bowl. Pour it on top of the rolls. Mix the sugar and lemon zest in a separate small bowl. Sprinkle half the sugar-lemon topping on top of the rolls and save the rest in the bowl for after baking.

8. **Bake and cool.** Bake for 17 to 20 minutes, or until the tops have browned and the dough is completely cooked through. The rolls are finished when the center is 195°F inside. Cool for 5 minutes on a heat-proof surface, until the rolls are cool enough to handle.

9. **Dip again in the topping.** Dip each roll in the bowl of topping to add an extra layer. Place the rolls on a cooling rack and allow them to cool for 15 to 20 minutes. Serve warm or at room temperature. Leftovers will stay fresh, tightly covered, for up to 3 days at room temperature.

EAT IT! Believe it or not, these are delicious when split in half and spread with butter. Try serving them with any springtime meal alongside a savory dish. Keep this recipe in mind for Mother's Day brunch!

Vanilla Sugar Pull-Apart Rolls

Yield 24 rolls Prep 20 minutes Inactive 2 hours 25 minutes
Bake 25 minutes

If you have whole vanilla beans, scrape out some of the inside and add it to the dough. You'll get a speckled, extra flavorful roll that will look almost like vanilla bean ice cream when you bite into it.

TOOLS:		
Large mixing bowl Rubber spatula Clean tea towel Plastic wrap	Small microwave-safe bowl Sharp knife	9-by-13-inch baking dish Baking sheet Parchment paper

For the dough

¾ cup water

5 tablespoons
(70 grams) unsalted
butter, softened

⅓ cup
(66 grams) white
sugar

3 cups (375 grams)
all-purpose flour

1½ teaspoons salt

2 teaspoons yeast,
instant or active dry

1 teaspoon vanilla
extract

1 vanilla bean
(optional)

Nonstick cooking spray

**For the vanilla
sugar topping**

¼ cup
(75 grams) butter

¾ cup
(150 grams) white
sugar

1 tablespoon vanilla

1. **Combine the dough ingredients.** Combine the water, butter, sugar, flour, salt, yeast, and vanilla in a large mixing bowl. The dough will be slightly sticky and will stick to the spatula and sides of the bowl as you mix. If you have a whole vanilla bean, scrape out the insides and add to the dough.

2. **Knead the dough.** Turn the dough out onto a clean, lightly floured counter, and knead for 7 to 10 minutes. As you knead, the dough will become less sticky. If the dough is too hard to work with, add 1 tablespoon of flour. Continue to knead until the dough feels soft, smooth, and elastic.

3. **The first rise.** Gently shape the dough into a ball and place it inside a large, lightly oiled mixing bowl. Cover the dough with a damp tea towel or plastic wrap and allow it to rise in a warm place for 1 hour to 1 hour, 30 minutes, or until it has doubled in size and is very puffy. Because this is an enriched dough, it may take extra time.

4. **Make the topping.** Melt ¼ cup of butter in a microwave-safe bowl. Add ¼ cup of sugar and vanilla and stir. The mixture will look like wet sand. Set aside while you divide and shape the rolls.

5. **Divide the dough.** Turn the dough out onto a clean countertop. Divide into 24 roughly equal pieces using a sharp knife. It is easiest to divide the dough in half, then quarters, then eighths. When you have eight pieces, divide each of them into three.

6. **Shape into rolls.** Line a baking sheet with parchment paper. Pick up one portion of dough and pinch the bottom to pull the top of the roll tight. You will see the roll become round and smooth on top as you pinch. Never smash down on the rolls from the top to shape them or they will be flat and dense.

7. **Roll in vanilla sugar mixture.** Coat the baking dish with cooking spray. Gently roll each ball of dough into the topping mixture until it is completely covered. Place the balls of dough in the baking dish spaced equally apart.

8. **The second rise.** Cover the baking dish with heavily greased plastic wrap, and place it in a warm place to rise again for 30 to 45 minutes, or until the rolls are almost touching. These are small rolls and will rise quickly. Halfway through the rising time, preheat your oven to 350°F with a rack in the center.

9. **Bake and cool.** Bake for 20 to 25 minutes, or until the tops have browned and the dough is completely cooked through. The rolls are finished when the center is 195°F inside. Remove the baking sheet from the oven, and allow the rolls to cool for 5 minutes, or until they are cool enough to handle.

Raspberry Jam Braided Sweet Bread

Yield 1 braided roll   Prep 20 minutes   Inactive 2 hours   Bake 30 minutes

This sweet bread is filled with raspberry jam and a cheesecake-like cream cheese filling. Even though there are a lot of steps, it's easy to put together. If you'd like to make this the day before to serve for breakfast, cover it with plastic wrap after it's fully assembled. Let it rest at room temperature for an hour in the morning before you bake.

TOOLS:		

Large mixing bowl
Rubber spatula
Clean tea towel
Plastic wrap
	Rolling pin
	Parchment
	  paper
	Baking sheet
		Sharp knife
		Electric mixer for the
		  filling

For the dough

½ cup water

4 tablespoons (57 grams) butter, softened

¼ cup (50 grams) sugar

2 teaspoons yeast, instant or active dry

1 egg

1 teaspoon vanilla

¾ teaspoon salt

2¾ cups (344 grams) all-purpose flour

For the filling and topping

8 ounces cream cheese, at room temperature

½ cup (100 grams) sugar

1 egg

¼ cup raspberry jam

Sparkling sugar, for topping

1. **Mix the dough ingredients.** In a large mixing bowl, combine the water, butter, sugar, yeast, egg, vanilla, salt, and flour. Use a spatula to make sure everything is fully incorporated. If the dough is very dry, slowly add a few teaspoons of water and keep mixing.

2. **Knead the dough.** Turn the dough out onto the counter and knead it for 7 to 10 minutes. It may feel slightly sticky at first, but it should become easier to work with as you knead. If it is sticking to your hands a lot, spray them with cooking spray and continue kneading.

Avoid adding more flour unless the dough is so wet that it's not forming a ball. Keep kneading until the dough is smooth and stretchy.

3. **The first rise.** Gently shape the dough into a smooth ball and place it inside a clean, lightly oiled bowl. Cover the dough with a damp tea towel or greased plastic wrap. Put it in a warm place to rise for 1 hour. It is done rising when it is doubled in size and very puffy.

4. **Make the filling.** Using an electric mixer, beat the cream cheese, sugar, and egg until smooth. (Make sure the cream cheese is at room temperature or it will not be smooth.) Set aside while you roll out the dough.

5. **Roll the dough.** Turn the dough out onto a lightly floured counter. Using a rolling pin, roll the dough out into a 10-by-15-inch rectangle. Line a baking sheet with parchment paper and place the dough in the center of it.

6. **Spread the filling.** Spread the cream cheese filling in a 4-inch-wide section down the center of the dough rectangle. This means you have 3-inch empty sections of dough on either side of the cream cheese. Spread the raspberry jam on top of the cream cheese filling.

7. **Cut the sides into strips.** Using a sharp knife, cut the empty sides into 2-inch horizontal strips. Cut off the top and bottom strip from each side. Gently stretch each strip diagonally across the center so you are making a series of XXs across the center of the loaf. If the dough tears, just pinch it back together and keep working. Gently press the dough along the edges where the strips meet the loaf to close the seams.

8. **The second rise.** Cover the loaf with greased plastic wrap, and put it in a warm place to rise again. This will take about 45 minutes to 1 hour. The loaf will not double in size but will be puffy. Toward the end of the rising time, preheat the oven to 375°F with the rack in the center.

continued ▶

9. **Add the topping and bake.** Sprinkle coarse sparkling sugar on top of the loaf and bake for 25 to 30 minutes, until golden brown. The internal temperature will be 195°F when the loaf is baked through. Cool the loaf on a wire rack for 20 minutes, then cut into slices and serve.

TRY THIS! Other flavors of jam will work well, too. Think of any flavor that goes well with cheesecake, and it will work well in this recipe.

KNEAD HELP? Is your braid looking a little messy? That is normal and okay! It will smooth out a bit as it rises and bakes. If you don't want to worry about making the braid, you can just fold the sides up and cut slashes in them, then pinch the top and bottom seams closed.

SOURDOUGHS AND STARTERS

We are really starting a new chapter in your bread-baking journey here. In a way, baking with sourdough is unlike anything you've done so far: there's no yeast, rise times are very long, and the dough is often very wet. At the same time, everything you've learned so far will come in handy as you learn to work with sourdough. You'll use the no-knead techniques you learned in chapter 2, work with steam in the oven, and add mix-ins to the dough. Sourdough has boomed in popularity in the past few years, so let's dive in and discover what the fuss is about.

The Foundation: Seven-Day Sourdough Starter

Yield 1 quart **Prep** 10 minutes per day **Inactive** 7 days

All sourdough recipes will have some sourdough starter as an ingredient. Sourdough starter is just a fermented blend of flour and water. In every recipe, it will make your bread rise and give it great tangy flavor. Amazingly, all you need to make your own starter is flour and water, along with one other crucial ingredient: time.

TOOLS:		
Two 1-quart size or larger nonreactive container, such as a widemouthed mason jar	Small spoon or rubber spatula Measuring cup or digital scale	Cotton tea towel or other piece of breathable fabric to cover the jar Rubber band

5 cups of filtered water, divided (each feeding will be about ¼ cup or 65 grams)

5 cups (625 grams) all-purpose flour, divided (each feeding will be about ½ cup or 65 grams)

1. **Day 1: Mix the water and flour.** Combine ½ cup of water and ¼ cup of flour in a 1-quart jar, and mix thoroughly. Cover the jar with a breathable fabric such as a cotton tea towel secured with a rubber band. Set it on the counter, out of direct sunlight or any drafts, and leave it alone for 24 hours. A warmer kitchen will help the process go faster.

2. **Day 2: Feed the starter.** After 24 hours, stir the starter and feed it again the exact same way (¼ cup of water plus ½ cup of flour). Stir very well until there are no visible bits of flour. Cover the jar and set it aside again for 24 hours.

3. **Day 3: Discard some starter and get a clean jar.** After another 24 hours, on the third day, the starter should look bubbly and may have separated into layers. It may also have developed an unpleasant smell. This is totally normal at this stage. (In the future, it should not smell bad, but for now it is normal.) Stir everything back together, then pour ½ cup of the starter into a new, clean jar. To this new jar, add ¼ cup of water and ½ cup of flour (your normal feeding) and stir well. Cover with the same breathable fabric and set aside.

4. **Day 4: Feed twice, discarding ½ cup before feedings.** On the fourth day, you will increase the feedings to twice a day. Before you feed the starter, mix it up well, pour ½ cup into a measuring cup, and dispose of it. Feed ¼ cup of water and ½ cup of flour in the morning and repeat at night, stirring well each time. After day 7, you will be able to use the discard for recipes, but for now, you will need to throw the excess starter away.

5. **Days 5 to 7: Repeat twice-daily feedings and discards.** For the next three days, feed your starter the same size feeding (¼ cup of water and ½ cup of flour). Before each feeding, mix up the starter and discard ½ cup of it.

6. **Check for maturity.** At the end of day 7, check to see if the starter is ready for baking. It should be visibly bubbly and have a sour smell. There are two ways to test to see if the starter is ready for baking. First is the float test: fill a glass with water and scoop a few table-spoons of starter on top. If it floats, you can bake with it. Another test is the doubling test. After feeding your starter, place a rubber band around the jar to mark its height. In 4 to 8 hours, if the volume of the starter doubles, you can bake with it.

7. **Maintain.** Once your starter has matured, you can reduce the feedings to once a day, continuing to discard each time. You can also store

continued ▶

the starter in the refrigerator and feed it once a week. If you notice a water layer on top, that just means the starter is hungry and could use an extra feeding.

KNEAD HELP? Wondering why you have to throw away so much starter? Great question. First, if you didn't, your starter would soon become too large for the jar. Second, disposing of some of the starter saves flour in the long run. That's because you are keeping your starter small, which means its feedings stay small. Sourdough starter needs a feeding that is the same size as itself to stay active. So, if your starter stays ½ cup in volume, it needs a ½-cup feeding. If you allow it to grow to 1 quart, it will need a 1-quart feeding each time.

Did you miss a feeding? That's okay. Do it when you remember, and pick right back up where you left off. Your starter can almost always be saved by feeding it more.

If your starter develops green, black, or pink mold, you need to throw it out. This is very, very unusual, but it does happen. Just toss it and try again.

EAT IT! You should never eat raw sourdough starter. However, you can bake with the discarded portion. It adds a tangy flavor to baked goods, similar to baking with sour cream or buttermilk. Search for sourdough discard recipes online for ideas.

Beginner's Sourdough Rustic Loaf

Yield 1 loaf   Prep 20 minutes   Inactive 32 hours   Bake 40 minutes

Sourdough bread has a reputation for being finicky, but this recipe is different. The dough is not wet and sticky like so many sourdough breads, so it's easy to work with and keeps its shape as it rises. You'll need to start this the day before you want to eat it.

TOOLS:		
Rubber band Large mixing bowl Rubber spatula	Tea towel 4- to 5-quart Dutch oven with a tight lid	Parchment paper Sharp knife or lame

For the sourdough starter

¾ cup (100 grams) all-purpose flour

½ cup (100 grams) water

For the bread dough

¾ cup (165 grams) fed sourdough starter

3½ cups (450 grams) bread flour

½ tablespoon (6 grams) sugar

1 cup lukewarm water

1¾ teaspoons salt

1. **Prepare the sourdough starter.** Discard half the starter and feed the remainder with ¾ cup (100 grams) flour and ½ cup (100 grams) water. (If the starter looks a little too thick, add a little more water; if the starter looks a little too liquidy, add a little more flour.) Mark the top with a rubber band, stir vigorously, and set aside until active, bubbly, and doubled in size. This will take from 4 to 8 hours, depending on the temperature of your room.

2. **Combine the ingredients.** Mix the bread flour, starter, sugar, and water in a large mixing bowl. Use your hands to make sure everything is incorporated into a ball. Cover the bowl with a damp tea towel and let it rest on the counter. (It helps to measure out the salt into a

continued ▶

separate container on place it on top of the towel so you don't forget to add it later.)

3. **Knead in the salt.** Turn the dough out onto a clean counter. Sprinkle half the salt on top of the dough, and start kneading to mix it in. Add the rest of the salt, and knead a few minutes more. Knead for about 4 to 5 minutes, or until the dough is soft and smooth and you can't feel any grittiness from the salt.

4. **The first rise.** Place the dough inside a clean, lightly oiled bowl, and cover it with a damp tea towel. Place it in a warm location to rise for 3 to 4 hours. The dough will increase in size, but it may be slow and may not double in size.

5. **Shape and the second rise.** Line a Dutch oven with parchment paper. Pick up the dough and gently shape it into a ball. Place it on top of the parchment paper inside the Dutch oven. If needed, press the paper down along the edges so it doesn't touch the dough. Cover the Dutch oven with the lid and place in the refrigerator overnight, from 8 to 16 hours.

6. **Bake.** In the morning, arrange your oven with a rack in the lower center, making sure there is enough height above the rack to allow you to place the Dutch oven inside with the lid on. Preheat the oven to 450°F. Remove the Dutch oven from the refrigerator. Rub the top of the loaf with flour, and slash down the center with a very sharp knife or lame. Put the lid back on. Bake the loaf for a total of 40 minutes: 20 minutes with the lid on, 20 minutes with the lid off.

7. **Cool.** Carefully remove the loaf from the Dutch oven and peel off the parchment paper if it has stuck to the bottom. Place the bread on a cooling rack and allow it to cool for 4 hours before slicing.

Chocolate and Orange Zest Sourdough Boule

Yield 1 loaf Prep 20 minutes Inactive 31 hours Bake 50 minutes

This recipe is higher hydration than the beginner sourdough loaf, so you'll want to have a proofing basket to help it hold its shape. If you like the open texture of this higher-hydration loaf, you can, of course, skip the mix-ins and make this as a regular sourdough bread.

TOOLS:		
Large mixing bowl Rubber spatula Clean tea towel Banneton (proofing basket)	Plastic wrap Parchment paper Sharp knife or lame	4- to 5-quart Dutch oven with a tight-fitting lid

For the sourdough starter

¾ cup (100 grams) all-purpose flour

½ cup (100 grams) water

For the bread dough

3½ cups (450 grams) bread flour

1⅓ cups lukewarm water

2 tablespoons (25 grams) white sugar

¾ cup (165 grams) mature well-fed sourdough starter

1¼ teaspoons salt

½ cup semisweet chocolate chunks

3 tablespoons freshly grated orange zest

Rice flour, for dusting

1. **Prepare your sourdough starter.** Discard half the starter and feed the remainder with ¾ cup (100 grams) flour and ½ cup (100 grams) water. Stir vigorously and set aside until active, bubbly, and doubled in size. This will take from 4 to 8 hours, depending on the temperature of your room.

2. **Combine the ingredients.** Combine the flour, water, sugar, and starter in a large bowl and stir. Use your hands to incorporate any dry bits. Cover the dough with a clean, damp tea towel and allow it to rest at room temperature for 30 minutes.

3. **Knead in the remaining ingredients.** After the rest period, add the salt, chocolate chunks, and orange zest. Knead for 1 to 2 minutes, or until everything is thoroughly combined. Cover the dough with a damp towel and allow it to rise in a warm place for 3 hours. Every hour, reshape the dough into a ball by folding it up. You can do this right in the bowl: simply grab each corner of the dough, pull it to the center, and turn it over so it looks like a ball again. When you come back 1 hour later, it will have lost its shape. That's okay; you are still building structure in the dough with each fold. You will reshape the dough three times. Immediately after you shape the dough a third time, it is time for the second rise.

4. **Second rise in a proofing basket.** Heavily dust a banneton with rice flour. When it is time to shape the dough the third time, place the loaf into the banneton and cover it with plastic wrap. Allow it to proof overnight in the refrigerator, for 8 to 16 hours.

5. **Bake.** In the morning, preheat the oven to 450°F with a rack in the center. Remove the dough from the refrigerator and turn it out onto a sheet of parchment paper, trying to have it land in the center. The dough may not have changed in size much overnight. This is perfectly fine; it will rise a lot in the oven. Score the top with a lame or very sharp knife. Place the parchment paper and dough into a lidded Dutch oven, and put the lid back on top. Bake for a total of 50 minutes: 25 minutes covered and 25 minutes uncovered. The loaf will be very brown and 200°F inside when it is done.

continued ▶

6. **Cool and serve.** Remove the loaf from the Dutch oven and remove the parchment paper. Allow the loaf to cool on a wire rack for 3 to 4 hours before slicing. This bread will stay fresh for 3 days, tightly wrapped, at room temperature.

KNEAD HELP? The chocolate may streak a little as you knead the dough. Make sure you're using chocolate chunks, not chocolate chips, to help with this. You can also try running your hands under cold water and drying them off before kneading any more. A little streaking is not a big deal, and your loaf will still look and taste lovely.

DON'T HAVE IT? If you don't have a Dutch oven, you can still bake this bread. The purpose of the Dutch oven is to create a high-humidity environment: the steam helps the dough rise higher. You can create steam in your oven on your own. When you're preheating the oven, put an empty rimmed metal baking sheet inside. Place the loaf on a separate parchment-paper-lined baking sheet. When you place the loaf inside, pour 1 cup of water onto the hot baking sheet to create steam.

Cheesy Sourdough Pull-Apart Bread

Yield 12 rolls   Prep 20 minutes   Inactive 16 hours   Bake 15 minutes

This cheesy, tangy pull-apart bread makes a great appetizer, side dish, or party starter!

TOOLS:		
Large mixing bowl Rubber spatula Tea towel	9-by-13-inch baking dish Sharp knife	Plastic wrap Small bowl Pastry brush

For the sourdough starter

¾ cup (100 grams) all-purpose flour

½ cup (100 grams) water

For the bread dough

1¼ cups (330 grams) sourdough starter

3 cups (375 grams) bread flour

¾ cup plus 1 tablespoon water

½ teaspoon (6 grams) sugar

1½ teaspoons salt

Nonstick cooking spray

4 tablespoons butter, melted

1 tablespoon dried parsley

1 teaspoon garlic powder

1 cup shredded cheddar cheese

1. **Prepare the sourdough starter.** Discard half the starter and feed the remainder with ¾ cup (100 grams) flour and ½ cup (100 grams) water. Stir vigorously and set aside until active, bubbly, and doubled in size. This will take from 4 to 8 hours, depending on the temperature of your room.

2. **Combine the ingredients.** Combine the starter, flour, water, and sugar in a large bowl. Stir to combine. The mixture should be a slightly sticky dough. Cover and allow to rest for between 20 and 40 minutes. (It helps to measure out the salt into a separate container and place it on top of the towel so you don't forget to add it later.)

3. **Knead in the salt.** Turn the dough out onto a clean counter. Sprinkle half the salt on top of the dough and start kneading to mix it in. Add the rest of the salt and knead for a few minutes more. Keep kneading for about 4 to 5 minutes, or until the dough is soft and smooth and you can't feel any grittiness.

4. **The first rise.** Place the dough inside a clean, lightly oiled bowl and cover it with a damp tea towel. Place it in a warm location to rise for 3 to 4 hours. This dough has a lot of starter in the recipe, so it should rise well and double in size within 4 hours.

5. **Divide and shape.** Prepare a 9-by-13-inch baking dish by spraying with nonstick cooking spray. Divide the dough into 12 equal pieces. First divide in half, then quarters, and each quarter into thirds. Using the palms of your hands, roll each piece gently into a ball. Arrange the rolls in the baking dish, equally spaced apart.

6. **The second rise.** Cover the dish with heavily greased plastic wrap and put it in a warm place to rise for 2 to 3 hours, until the rolls are very puffy and are almost touching. Toward the end of the rising time, preheat your oven to 375°F with the rack in the center.

7. **Score.** Using a sharp knife, score each roll diagonally through the center.

8. **Prepare the topping.** Mix the melted butter, parsley, and garlic powder in a small bowl. Brush it on top of the rolls, being careful not to squish them. If there is any extra, drizzle it on top.

9. **Bake and serve.** Bake for 15 minutes, until the rolls are partially baked. Sprinkle on the cheddar cheese, and bake for 10 minutes more, until the bread is baked through and the cheese is browned. Allow the rolls to cool for 5 to 10 minutes in the baking dish, and serve them warm.

Swirled Cinnamon Raisin Sourdough

Yield 1 loaf Prep 20 minutes Inactive 18 hours Bake 50 minutes

This soft sandwich loaf is the perfect blend of tangy sourdough flavor and sweet cinnamon sugar and raisins. A slice of this bread feels cozy and comforting on a chilly morning. It's our tradition to make it on snow days.

TOOLS:		
Large mixing bowl Rubber spatula Small bowl	Tea towel 8½-by-4½-by- 2½-inch loaf pan	Plastic wrap

For the sourdough starter

¾ cup (100 grams) all-purpose flour

½ cup (100 grams) water

For the bread dough

¾ cup (165 grams) active sourdough starter

3 cups (375 grams) all-purpose flour

¼ cup (57 grams) butter, softened

¼ cup (49 grams) brown sugar

⅔ cup milk

1 egg

½ cup raisins

1½ teaspoons salt

For the cinnamon sugar filling

¼ cup (50 grams) granulated sugar

1 tablespoon cinnamon

For assembly

1 egg, beaten

1. **Prepare the sourdough starter.** Discard half the starter and feed the remainder with ¾ cup (100 grams) flour and ½ cup (100 grams) water. Stir vigorously and set aside until active, bubbly, and doubled in size. This will take from 4 to 8 hours, depending on the temperature of your room.

2. **Combine the ingredients.** Combine the flour, starter, butter, brown sugar, milk, and egg in a large mixing bowl until a slightly dry, shaggy dough is formed. The dough will become smoother as you knead and the butter is incorporated, so don't add any additional liquid yet. Cover the dough with a clean tea towel and allow it to rest at room

temperature for about 30 minutes. Meanwhile, submerge the raisins in warm water, and set aside to soak. (Don't skip the step of soaking the raisins, or they will pull moisture from the bread dough, leaving you with dry spots in your loaf.)

3. **Knead the dough, and add the raisins.** Add the salt and knead the dough by hand or with an electric stand mixer for 5 to 7 minutes, until a smooth and soft dough forms. If the dough seems very dry, looks crumbly, or is not forming a ball, add 1 tablespoon or so more of milk. If it seems too wet and is sticking to the sides of the bowl or to the counter, add more flour, 1 tablespoon at a time. The dough is ready to shape when it reaches the windowpane stage, meaning that when a golf ball–size piece of dough is stretched out, translucent areas appear. Drain the raisins, add them to the dough, and gently knead until they are evenly distributed through the dough.

4. **The first rise.** Place the dough inside a clean, lightly oiled bowl, cover it with a damp tea towel, and place it in a warm place to rise until nearly doubled in size, about 3 to 4 hours. (The time for this can vary depending on the strength of your starter and the warmth of your home.)

5. **Add the filling and shape.** Stretch the dough into a long rectangle, with the short side of the rectangle as long as the short side of the loaf pan. The longer your rectangle, the more swirls you will have. Mix the granulated sugar and cinnamon, and sprinkle onto the dough, leaving a 1-inch border in all directions. Fold in the top corners, or "shoulders," of the rectangle, then keep rolling tightly to form a log. Roll as tightly as you can. The tighter you roll, the more swirls you'll have. Pinch all seams shut and place the loaf seam-side down into a greased loaf pan.

continued ▶

6. **The second rise.** Cover the dough with heavily greased plastic wrap and allow it to rise again in a warm place for about 3 hours, until the loaf is one inch above the top of the loaf pan. (This may take longer, depending on your sourdough starter.) Toward the end of the rising time, preheat the oven to 350°F with the rack in the center. Brush the top of the loaf with the beaten egg.

7. **Bake and cool.** Remove the plastic wrap and bake for 40 to 50 minutes, until the loaf is deep golden brown and the internal temperature is 200°F. Remove it from the pan and allow it to cool for at least 1 hour before slicing. For the neatest slices, allow the bread to cool completely, for at least 3 hours. The bread will stay fresh at room temperature a few days, or frozen for up to 2 months.

KNEAD HELP? Like most sourdough recipes, this bread has long rising times. If you don't want to do it all in one day, you can pop the dough or shaped loaf into the refrigerator before the last rise and pick it up again in the morning.

TRY THIS! For extra crunch and flavor, add chopped walnuts to the cinnamon sugar.

EAT IT! Cinnamon raisin bread makes delicious French toast. If you have leftovers, cut them into thick slices and freeze for later. You can have homemade French toast at a moment's notice!

MEASUREMENT CONVERSIONS

VOLUME EQUIVALENTS

	U.S. STANDARD	U.S. STANDARD (OUNCES)	METRIC (APPROXIMATE)
LIQUID	2 tablespoons	1 fl. oz.	30 mL
	¼ cup	2 fl. oz.	60 mL
	½ cup	4 fl. oz.	120 mL
	1 cup	8 fl. oz.	240 mL
	1½ cups	12 fl. oz.	355 mL
	2 cups or 1 pint	16 fl. oz.	475 mL
	4 cups or 1 quart	32 fl. oz.	1 L
	1 gallon	128 fl. oz.	4 L
DRY	⅛ teaspoon		0.5 mL
	¼ teaspoon		1 mL
	½ teaspoon		2 mL
	¾ teaspoon		4 mL
	1 teaspoon		5 mL
	1 tablespoon		15 mL
	¼ cup		59 mL
	⅓ cup		79 mL
	½ cup		118 mL
	⅔ cup		156 mL
	¾ cup		177 mL
	1 cup		235 mL
	2 cups or 1 pint		475 mL
	3 cups		700 mL
	4 cups or 1 quart		1 L
	½ gallon		2 L
	1 gallon		4 L

OVEN TEMPERATURES

FAHRENHEIT	CELSIUS (APPROXIMATE)
250°F	120°C
300°F	150°C
325°F	165°C
350°F	180°C
375°F	190°C
400°F	200°C
425°F	220°C
450°F	230°C

WEIGHT EQUIVALENTS

U.S. STANDARD	METRIC (APPROXIMATE)
½ ounce	15 g
1 ounce	30 g
2 ounces	60 g
4 ounces	115 g
8 ounces	225 g
12 ounces	340 g
16 ounces or 1 pound	455 g

Breadtopia: Breadtopia.com

This website has an online shop, recipes, a blog, and even a forum where you can connect and discuss bread baking with other bakers.

Heart's Content Farmhouse: HeartsContentFarmhouse.com

As you continue baking with sourdough, you'll need more recipes for sourdough discard. My website has dozens with step-by-step photos and videos.

King Arthur Flour: KingArthurBaking.com

This online shop stocks tools and ingredients, all tailored to bakers. You'll be able to find any tools you need, as well as high-quality flour. They have an extensive website and a print catalog you can request.

The Perfect Loaf: ThePerfectLoaf.com

If you find yourself in love with sourdough and want to look for more information, this website has many advanced sourdough techniques and recipes.

Pleasant Hill Grain: PleasantHillGrain.com

This shop stocks affordable bread-baking tools such as proofing baskets, lames, and loaf pans. They have a live chat on their website that will help you find exactly what you need.

INDEX

ABOUT THE AUTHOR

 Katie Shaw lives in Virginia on a 9-acre hobby farm with her husband and three daughters. She is the writer and photographer behind the food and homesteading blog HeartsContentFarmhouse.com, where she shares recipes for bread, soap, and other kitchen projects.

Katie is a self-taught baker who loves to make things as simple as possible. She believes that if you can read, you can bake.

You can find her on YouTube at YouTube.com/heartscontentfarmhouse or Instagram at @heartscontentfarmhouse.